Published by Little Toller Books in 2017
Little Toller Books, Lower Dairy, Toller Fratrum, Dorset

Words © Fiona Sampson 2017

The right of Fiona Sampson to be identified as the author of this work
has been asserted by her in accordance with Copyright, Design and
Patents Act 1988

We have made every effort to trace the copyright-holders; in the event of an
inadvertent omission or error please notify Little Toller Books

Jacket artwork © Zoran Mušič courtesty of Fondazione Gabriele e
Anna Braglia, Lugano. Photograph by Christoph Münstermann

Typeset by Little Toller Books

Printed by TJ International, Padstow, Cornwall

All papers used by Little Toller Books are natural, recyclable products made
from wood grown in sustainable, well-managed forests

A catalogue record for this book is available from the British Library

ISBN 978-1-908213-51-8

01

Limestone Country

FIONA SAMPSON

A LITTLE TOLLER **MONOGRAPH**

For Peter

Contents

Introduction

This book is about a love affair with limestone, that sedimentary rock, largely calcium carbonate, which time and water make out of bones and shells. Limestone is the cannibal earth reconsuming her own. But its lacy spume is a hundred times more delicate than marble.

Seventeen years ago I moved to the west of Oxfordshire, where that county meets Gloucestershire and Wiltshire, and found myself living for the first time in a limestone landscape. Our home was built of the curiously friable local stone. The same stone lay everywhere in the furrows of fields around us. Twice a year, ploughing turned up chunks that were chock-full of fossils, a tangible reminder of how we rose out of the sea, are seven-tenths water – and will probably eventually be resubmerged by our own environmental wilfulness. Our old farmworker's cottage was about as far inland as it's possible to get in Britain; yet we lived at sea-level, where every spring the water rose higher in the ditches and lay for longer in the fields.

This misty waterland is just one kind of limestone country. Limestone dazzles in Sicily, contorts the highlands of Bosnia, paves The Burren in County Clare, emerges in fantastical tufa formations on the eastern Mediterranean, in Lebanon and Israel, and creates the dramatic caves and gorges of karst regions like Slovenia's Kras, the Chocolate Hills of the Philippines – or Australia's Nullarbor Plain. Rome is built from Travertine limestone. Mount Parnassus is limestone, as is the pavement of the Acropolis.

Many of these are among my favourite places. It was a shock, and an epiphany, to realise that they are all made from – and in and on – limestone. Surely, I thought, this has to be more than mere coincidence. I realised that, varied as they are, they share a particular plasticity. Limestone has a special relationship with water, by which it's shaped at every stage of its existence. The dreamtime of limestone is the long era of its sedimentary laying down, in the saltwater of seas so lost that they seem almost imaginary: Pannonia, the Niobraran. Even once it has been deposited, limestone remains malleable and soluble. It is water, not fire, that creates its strata, rift-like valleys and rolling plateaux. Water will always find ways through, and in doing so creates a landscape of springs and rivers, yet also of plateaux from which all the surface water has been drained away.

Subtle, water-inflected, still ceaselessly in transition, limestone is welcoming to humans, who have long found it adapts easily to their needs, as they to it. It enabled some of the earliest human settlement and art of which we know. The great paintings of Lascaux and other nearby caves, which date from 15,000 BCE, are found in the limestone valley of the River Vézère, in France. A few kilometres further south again, the inhabitants of the limestone Grotte du Vallonnet left their tools behind over 1,000,000 BCE.

The *dolines*, or bowl-shaped valleys that limestone characteristically creates, whether in Périgord or in the winegrowing west of Slovenia, invite cultivation and settlement. They also invite the outdoor shrines that survive widely on the European continent. Reminders of the earliest human psychogeography, these grottoes, springs and declivities, first dedicated to a *deus loci* long before the advent of the Romans who coined that term, are still with us: often disguised by rededication, frequently for example to the Virgin Mary. Perhaps the Pennine-born poet W. H. Auden was right, when he claimed, in his poem 'In Praise of Limestone', that 'when I try to imagine a faultless love / Or the life to come, what I hear is the murmur / Of underground streams, what I see is a limestone landscape'.

Now that we've moved to a small farm on the banks of the River Auvézère in Périgord, where we live for half the year, I find myself unable to forget his words. This wooded landscape of *dolines* and *causses*, or high ridges, is interrupted only by mediaeval hamlets built in brilliant-white limestone, and by the small fields and orchards of family farms. It's easy to see how this environment produces the ways we live in it. To stand on high ground and gaze out as far as the eye can see is to understand *how it works*.

An observer who, like me, has no poem to write might put the case for limestone exceptionalism more simply. Geology is present in our daily life (most palpably so, I'll admit, outside cities and suburbs) because it generates a particular ecology; and that ecology in turn generates quite specific forms of human life. Of course, climate plays a part in this too; and so does human history. But which came first, geography or history? And where does one end and the other begin?

Our Oxfordshire village once stood in the path of the English Civil War, and was later used as an experiment in the Agricultural Revolution. Mediaeval Périgord was the cradle of the Hundred Years' War. The Karst region of western Slovenia, where I've made repeated visits to the village of Škocjan in search of another possible life, and where I set the summer quarter of this book, was the scene of one of the most brutal fronts of the First World War, and was occupied by Italy from 1920 to 1945. And Jerusalem, that limestone city in a limestone landscape, has been so intensely imagined through the centuries by the Abrahamic religions that its story has been one of almost ceaseless tragedy, cyclical destruction and occupation.

Really living in these landscapes means paying radical attention to how they behave. It means knowing their wildlife as well as ways of farming, observing how water and vegetation respond to the mineral facts of rock and soil as much as how humans live in and with them. The family farmers of Périgord, the villagers of Slovenia – where patterns of land ownership were changed by the 'soft' communism of Yugoslavia, but farming methods were not – and British organic farmers all know their locality deeply, even profoundly; in a way that the absentee managers of agribusinesses, for example, cannot. Such attention is patient and detailed. It's a kind of 'slow knowledge' that is the opposite of generalisation.

And I have tried not to generalise. If my first three limestone landscapes are all European, that's simply because they are the ones that I know best, and mean most to me. This book isn't, after all, a karstological survey of the world's limestone phenomena, but my own personal exploration of limestone country. Life, even in such landscapes, is messy with overlaps and repetitions: which I have simplified. I want to juxtapose the differences between these places, not join them up and homogenise them. To try and make them 'read' separately, I have also reversed the order of the seasons. Instead of starting with spring and all that leads to, I've begun with autumn and worked backwards to arrive at winter.

It's in winter that I visit Jerusalem – that famous, notorious city much dreamt of in each of the book's other locations, as it is across the world – to look for a different way of understanding how a limestone landscape can enter the imagination. After all, how can we separate what a place *is* from what it is *for us*? Places are meanings, as well as conditions. They act upon us, and we act upon them, in the dialectic we call *living*. This is a book about trying on possible ways of living – or dying – in limestone country; about candidates for Auden's 'faultless love'.

Autumn
Le Chambon

Santat!

The Savignacs are in the kitchen when we arrive for *un petit apéro*. The stove is lit and, with all five of them already crowded round the table, there's hardly space for us. Heat; noise. Here's Jeannot, the paterfamilias, hitching up his trousers below his belly. As he has no waist it's a hopeless and endless task that's become his signature gesture. Here's Madame Savignac, monumental and frowning with friendship. At our insistence she doesn't rise from her chair in the centre of the circle. And here is Clarette, with little Josette on her knee. Clarette is the one who got away, the educated daughter who works at the *Mairie*. She retains a frank bossiness that comes straight off the farm, but her daughter Josette, who's only three, is charmingly, excessively shy. The little girl can hardly bear to speak in our company, and she hides her face in her mother's jacket when we try to talk to her.

Finally, our special friend Nicolas is the grown-up son of the family. In his late thirties, with his father's long, slightly moony face and markedly un-moony temperament, he vibrates with good humour – and with furies that we hear arrive suddenly, and leave as quickly, when he and his father go yelling round the yard. And underfoot as always is Nicolas's beautiful collie, Jazz, prince of the hamlet pack. He rushes in and out the door looking for ways to impress us, until Nicolas loses patience and bundles him outside to play with our dogs.

While Clarette and Maman try to get the cat off the table, Nicolas and his father talk us through the relative virtues of the drinks on offer. They greatly enjoy a single malt, but they also have Pernod and homemade red wine, *vin de noix* and the *bernache* that so upset my stomach last time we visited: I hadn't realised it was the first pressing wine that we call *must*. We decide on *vin de noix* and, after Clarette has brought in an extra chair from the *arrière-cuisine*, the back kitchen, we settle down for an evening of talk.

Everyone in this generous, gregarious family talks at once. It's the biggest strain on British manners I've encountered since we got here. I'm still not confident with the rules of gender courtesy. When both speak at once, should I listen to Madame, or to Monsieur? It doesn't help that P, having little French, is unable to take up the slack. I slide from one interlocutor to the other. It would be bad enough in English, but at least I'd be lighter on my feet. Madame is explaining the provenance of the cat, whose mother and grandmother were also mousers on the farm, while Nicolas and Clarette want us to adjudicate the merits of their respective mobile-phone providers. I'm not sure about the etiquette of this debate either: instead I launch the unifying topic of difficulties with landline providers. Mercifully, everyone gets behind this and, in a moment of conversational calm, Jeannot slides our tumblers across the oilcloth.

Now we all have a drink in our hands – little Josette has

her beaker of juice – we raise our glasses to each other in a toast: Your health! *Santat!* For this is Périgord, and the family are speaking not French but Occitan. More, I'm falling in love with their language. For even in trivia Occitan seems to me somehow tastier – thicker and closer to the textures of actual life – than the stately measures of standard French.

But thick and tasty as their language may be, the Savignacs' *vin de noix* is thicker and tastier. It's brown and viscous, syrupy without being too sweet, with a tobacco taste of walnuts. It's also very strong. After two gulps I can feel it going to my head. Of course: this is really a fortified wine. Jeannot stood some of the farm's own Bergerac on macerated green walnuts – also from the family's own orchards – all summer, adding sugar and a little brandy to make a drink that must be at least 20 per cent proof. Every year he produces dozens of bottles of the stuff, and sells them in the local markets.

I take another mouthful. *Vin de noix* is delicious, and deliciously complicated. The grape flavours of the base wine haven't been burnt out as they would be if it were reduced to spirits. This is still wine; it's simply been overlaid with a tarry tang of walnut.

Meanwhile, the kitchen keeps getting hotter and noisier. Chicken bones bubble in a fatty broth on the stove. The cat's back on the table, being pushed away by Clarette in what's really a game. Nicolas has become flushed and is repeating that we need to have a bonfire. All those *branca*, branches of lime and ash, that P cut down yesterday: it's a waste to leave them to rot! Jeannot's talking to P – in hand gestures – about cars. Josette has slipped down from her mother's knee and is swinging on the door handle. Madame and I try to understand each other's recipes for chicken stock, but the wine's making my concentration unravel and I find it harder and harder to carry on our bilingual Franco-Occitan. Just when I think I simply must go home and lie down, Jeannot refills our glasses. *Santat!*

One Day

Our bedroom window overlooks the Savignacs' yard. Three cement barns stand in a loose circle between their house and ours. Each one is painted a creamish pink and each is kept neatly padlocked. The yard itself is partly cemented, partly gravelled. In the centre where cement and gravel meet is a large drain, whose rattling cover announces every arrival.

The window shutter has a swivel handle. All night it stays folded in the darkness between glazing and wood like a long bronze insect. When you open the window inward and reach through to take hold of this handle, it makes a satisfying, barely audible *clunk-click*, and the shutter is released to swing back against the outside wall with a hollow *plunk* of pine against limestone. You have to reach out and round to secure it with a metal peg set in the stonework wall, which holds it open the way page holders flatten a musical score.

This sound – the sound of wooden shutters swinging back one after another against the house wall – is what wakes me most mornings. It means P's opening up the house and waking the day. Under our heap of blankets I open my eyes experimentally. Still dark. I wait. Now the shutters in the next room go. A little light enters the doorway. I struggle to sit up, checking my breath on the air of the bedroom. Yes, it makes a misty cloud – still early, then.

In fact it's barely dawn. When P opens the bedroom shutters he reveals a velvety blue sky. In the west, over the river, it's still night. Only to the east, between the Savignacs' barns, can we see a smudge of purplish pink. It seems impossible that this could become heat and light. The night-freeze hangs in the air, misting the yard romantically. A white frost stands on every surface, delineating the lumpy stones of our garden wall, the corrugated lines of the tiled roofs.

Now the dogs rush in and leap on the bed to tell me all about it. Their fur smells of fresh air, like laundry that's been dried outdoors. P follows with our morning coffee. There's a brief tussle as he gets back into bed: dogs have to be admonished. Dusha, emotional as only a collie-lurcher cross can be, leans crestfallen against the footboard. Zoi – pure hound, pure id – licks P's face with her usual placatory cheer.

Meanwhile, out in the misty yard, there's a clatter and rumble as the concertina doors of the first barn are unlocked. This is where the Savignacs keep their mobile poultry shop. Cousin to an ice-cream stall or a kebab van, it has a side hatch that folds down to become a counter; when Monsieur Savignac mans this he towers above his customers, his head nudging the vehicle's ceiling. The van is cream-coloured, and embellished with blue signage – *M. J. Savignac, poules et dindes* – in a dashing diagonal cursive that has begun to fade. It is also often just a little dusty.

Today is Thursday, which means prepping for tomorrow's market in Excedeuil. But not just yet. First, the early morning arcana. The Savignacs are up every day before dawn, in summer not long after four, and start their yard work in the pre-dawn twilight. Today's no exception. Dimly, in the pinkish-grey light beginning to trickle across the field behind them, we make out Nicolas and Jeannot. It's Nicolas who's hauled the barn door open. He's still standing with his hand on the handle, apparently lost in thought, watching his father who is a dark mass in the shadow of the barn opposite.

Much of the Savignacs' farming day involves fiddling with machinery. As well as the mobile shop they have a small red tractor, the kind we used to draw when we were kids: two big wheels at the back, two small ones at the front, and an open cab. They also own a tractor with no cab at all; the driver, strapped to nothing, jounces around on what looks suspiciously like a bicycle saddle. In the far barn their giant green harvester, of which they're justly proud, sits mighty and modern waiting for its annual deployment. In various *granges*, sheds and nameless outbuildings dotted around the farm there are also chainsaws, hedge-trimmers, pumps and pesticide sprays innumerable: these are elderly, hard-worked pieces of kit, which have to be cajoled and bullied into performing properly. This morning is no exception. The last leaves on the yard's chestnut tree dangle like streamers against the pinkish white of the rising sun as Jeannot and his son disappear together into the tractor shed.

It's just after seven. P and I chat about our day. The mist in the barnyard is apricot-coloured now. Streaks of light are appearing in the sky to south and west. The window at the foot of our bed looks out onto a tangle of trees in the neighbours' garden. At dawn, even this late in autumn, they're noisy with birdsong. A blackbird calls, all liquid invention; another responds from close by. Woodpigeons, waking as the dark lifts, utter protesting moans and little endearing flutings. Somewhere close by a woodpecker starts up its neurotic drill.

As the light continues to grow, individual branches become visible. Closest is the dark green of the pine. Its twigs are like swags of fabric. Beyond them we can see the yellow foliage of an apple tree and next to it a plum. The sky behind them is all the colours of a healing bruise.

Seven-thirty. P jogs my elbow. Here swaying on the nearest branch is a red squirrel, carrying a nut like a saint his symbol, and regarding us assessingly. We hold our breaths. If it jumps in the room the dogs will have it. If we move to scare it off the dogs will notice that too and Zoi, at least, may try to throw herself through the window after it.

Then something happens in the farmyard – someone drops something with a clatter and yell – and everyone moves at once. The squirrel races away up the tree, the dogs rise yelling from the bed to rush between the windows, and P leaps up after them shouting at them to get downstairs.

By now the window above the yard is a square of apricot light. In the small pane on the opposite wall, the roof ridge of the barn makes a reticulated line drawn diagonally through the lifting gloom. The smell of P's second cup of coffee rises up the stairs, together with the seething sound of the percolator: our tile-floored kitchen makes everything echo. The radio sounds hollow-voiced, oracular. Dusha's and Zoi's claws click and slide. I can hear every word as P explains to them how much he needs this second dose of caffeine.

It's time to get up anyway. The house has a stone stoop at what's now first-floor level. We're so inured to hamlet life that we've developed the habit of sitting out here wrapped in dressing gowns, coats and blankets to eat our breakfast. In Le Chambon dressing decently simply means covering yourself up; it has nothing to do with smartness. Greeting the *facteur* in your dressing gown, or a raincoat over pyjamas, or ancient trousers held up with string, is not simply acceptable but absolutely normal.

It's funny, I think as I button my sheepskin over a pair of P's pyjamas and an old sweater, how dress codes take one step along. Here, women's housecoats aren't what you'd be embarrassed to be caught out wearing as they are in, say, a provincial city like Périgueux. Instead they're what you change *into* when you know someone's coming to visit. Rather than protecting your smart clothes from housewifely mess, they're the smart garment you slip over your personal messiness. So next door, in the kitchen of the hamlet's most prosperous farm, Madame Savignac daily dons her housecoat – just when a town housewife would take it off – to sit down to lunch and for the evening *apéro*.

Remember how embarrassed I was by the dressing gowns, I tell P. He laughs. He knows that I'm remembering the first time we called on our other neighbours. We wanted to thank Michel and Marie for the foie gras they'd given us. It was about five in the afternoon. We arrived with a bottle of wine and, lifting the latch twine, slipped through the rusty yard gate while fending off Suzi, the farm's *deus loci*. This was complicated because, if Jazz is the prince of the hamlet's dogs, Suzi is their reigning queen. She is to some extent a collie, but her father was clearly something black, shorthaired and shorter-tempered. She doesn't like our dogs, since both are bitches, and she has a small coterie of supporters who join her in policing the U-shaped lane that leads to her riverside home. Whenever she sees us, or if she's commanded to *Sesètz!* by old Michel, she crouches as if to pounce, all coiled energy. Though she's never attacked a human, I wouldn't trust her with livestock.

Luckily, Michel and Marie don't keep sheep or cattle. Their smallholding really is old-fashioned subsistence farming. They grow vegetables in a strip that looks like a mediaeval holding and leads down to the river; this is the extent of their *bien*, or property. Their barn has an open drying gallery for maize and peppers, below is the goose shed, and the whole elderly oak-frame structure leans sideways is if it longs to slide into the river. Sometimes we hear Michel and Marie's geese calling as we sit on our stoop; sometimes we see the birds wandering their yard in twos and threes. Like almost everyone in the hamlet, Marie makes and cans her own foie gras; but her geese aren't crated or force-fed.

Perhaps that's because now, in her seventies, she can't really be bothered. There's something of the sleepwalker about Marie; she's already confided that, while she likes talking to friends, she can't stand social gatherings. Michel is dreamy in a different way. With his white hair and rosy cheeks he looks as though he's stepped out of some old-fashioned propaganda about peasant life. Every afternoon around four o'clock we see him wander back from the bridge with Suzi, at his heel, crouching and feinting as she passes the neighbourhood cats and dogs. Marie speaks little; Michel, who's very deaf, speaks even less. So that afternoon when he opened the door to greet us, rather than speak, he smiled – with something approaching astonishment. The day was done. The remains of supper were on the table behind him. The old couple were both in their dressing gowns.

We were even more astonished. Yet there was nothing any of us could do but carry on. So we stepped into the dark kitchen where the table, standing before a huge smoke-blackened *cheminée*, was covered with the inevitable oilcloth and the floor was patched with aged lino of various designs. Moving their plates aside, our hosts invited us to sit down. Michel went to a cupboard in the wall and brought out some *vin de noix* while Marie, bending stiffly in a pink quilted nylon dressing gown – very like one I remember my mother wearing in the Seventies – brought out from some low cupboard four tumblers, their glass shrouded with scratches.

We settled down to talk. Michel and Marie seemed especially interested in the English climate. It's a phenomenon our neighbours here return to repeatedly. If you live much of your life outdoors, relying on the weather for your livelihood and indeed to feed you, this is not a trivial topic but one that goes to the heart of daily life. The Savignacs often ask us about the English *brume* (school textbooks across Europe seem to translate 'cloud' as 'fog'). So does the widow Paulette, who lives on the other side of the hamlet in a modern chalet – where she's placed her potted tomato plants at exact intervals along the veranda.

What our neighbours are really asking is: What must it be like to *live* there? They come at this slowly, deliberatingly, as something that must be got straight. We explain as best we can about the Gulf Stream and the rain; then we astonish them with how early it gets dark in December. At this all make the same sceptical gesture. They tuck their chins in and smile, watching our expressions for signs that we're having them on. Even Michel and Marie, awkward and dressing-gowned in their dark kitchen, tucked in their chins at us and laughed.

This morning, as we sit on the stoop stirring our porridge with hot spoons, it's a different, early morning *brume* that's dispersing over the river. Steam hangs above our bowls. A dog barks beyond the river. Two rooks rise vertically in the still air, then topple into treetops on the further bank. The sky, now entirely pink and pale blue, is the colours of a Baroque fresco.

It's quieter on this side of the house, away from the birdcage tangle of our neighbours' trees; in any case the dawn chorus is beginning to dissolve as the morning warms up. Instead we hear the isolated, almost tentative clinks and raps that reveal how the hamlet starts its day. A door opens somewhere. A car drones along the lane from the bridge. A dog bowl is dropped with a bright metallic *tang!* A snatch of children's voices from the schoolteachers' house: abruptly cut off as a window or a door is slammed shut. Someone knocking out the ashes riddled from the overnight stove. Someone, Michel or Marie, coughing down by the river. The distant snarl of a chainsaw at work somewhere in the woods.

In the stillness the sound of our own spoons chinking our porridge bowls carries too. I glance down and notice Jazz is at our gate, expressing his interest. He stands on hind legs to thread his muzzle between the bars of its nineteenth-century ironwork. Zoi races downstairs to greet him. The two dogs sniff and rub noses. At our feet, Dusha yawns and rolls onto her side. *Jazz, Jazz*, Nicolas yells from the yard. He appears behind his dog, overall-ed and carrying a huge spanner. *N'i a pas cap problèma?* he yells, waving hello. P, at the gate to let Jazz in, waves in return. *Pas de problème*, I yell back, as if we were facing each other across some vast river, not merely a grassy track. Jazz bounds into our yard, enquires rudely of our porridge bowls, skitters indoors. We hear a scutter and yap as our dogs join in his game.

Meanwhile Jeannot is waving from the far side of the orchard, where a quince tree marks the entrance to the poultry run. The Savignacs have a huge earthen yard, somewhere between half an acre and an acre of it, fenced in on every side with chicken wire three metres high. However efficiently business-like this compound may have appeared when it was new – fifty? sixty? years ago – by now it's invitingly informal. It's filled with old wooden arks, perches of various heights worn smooth as driftwood by the decades, and a maze of low, collapsing wire fences that must once have kept birds of different breeds apart from each other. The ground is littered with late windfall quinces that have been bruised and pecked open.

Turning, Jeannot disappears behind a visual fog of rolled and sagging wire, but we know that he's releasing his chickens, turkeys and guinea fowl from their overnight roosts. Sure enough, a wall of poultry sound starts up as they flock out into the daylight. The turkeys honk their morning announcements. The guinea fowl make the noise – like rusty chains, squealing wheels or a handsaw squeaking through fresh timber – that it took me several weeks to realise was the birds themselves, not some iterative old machinery. As well as these calls we hear the teeming chatter that all birds make when large numbers are preening together at one end of the day or the other.

In all this din Jeannot's voice doesn't carry well enough for us to hear what he's saying. It's a singsong that sounds as though he's greeting the birds or lulling them. But then there's the struggle and squawk that says one has just been dispatched. After a pause, it happens again – and again – and then again. This doesn't seem to me too bad a way to go: still half asleep and not yet awake to panic. The rest of the flock carry on fussing and calling as if nothing were happening. And as we put down our bowls we see Jeannot step out of the run, a dozen *poules* dangling from his arm.

Jazz must be able to smell them from here – or he knows the routine by heart – for now he's at the gate whining to be let out. After I've released him I go back into the kitchen, and find P nursing the fire. Rebuilding it in the embers works well, providing the logs we put on just before bed are large enough to burn till morning. Last night we must have judged this perfectly; our reward is a stove whose iron firebox is warm enough to help this morning's twigs spring alight. Now, testing the weight of each for dryness, P builds a criss-cross of narrow logs set loosely to take up the flames. When the fire's going strongly he shuts the stove door on its snoring sound, and goes upstairs to work.

By the time we take the dogs for their morning walk about an hour later, the pattern of the day is set. The schoolteachers and their kids have left for town. Paulette's granddaughter, who works in the Super-U about twelve kilometres away, has caught her lift. Michel has walked Suzi to the river and is dawdling home, pausing to lean on his stick and eye the tares in the field beside the swimming hole. I still need a scarf doubled around my throat but the day's sunny now; it's a glittery light that catches the tinfoil bird-scarer in the schoolteachers' plum tree, the white stones that mark the corners of the *pétanque* pitch, the glisten on the dogs' noses. We walk smartly to the swimming hole. A low skim of mist still hangs over the fields on either side of the track. The chill deepens as we get closer to the water; I'm shivering by the time we slither down onto the pebbled shore of the ford.

The dogs love it here. While they busy themselves in the swimming hole, P and I stroll the isthmus of pebbles looking for ceramic fragments. Recently, while tidying the barn, I found an earthenware walnut-oil jug, an altogether non-culinary object standing nearly a metre tall. Its glaze is a swirl of dark green, and the handles that support its neck are decorated with raised circles that look like octopus suckers but are really thumbprints in the pastry-crust of the raw clay. We speculated for some time: could it be a jar for storing grain? Or wine? Then the internet told me this was a Périgordian tradition, and that all such vessels can be dated to the eighteenth century because by the nineteenth they'd been replaced by tin and zinc and imported lighting fuel. Strange to imagine that the house used to be lit by walnut-oil lamps: it must have been suffocatingly aromatic.

The air under the trees fringing the River Auvézère smells as fresh as it is cool. As we stroll and poke, searching for the dark green of this local pottery among the dark-green waterweeds, the thawing earthen bank beside us gives off a clean clay smell. The paddling dogs kick up a faint, greenish aroma from the riverbed. Clustered keys from the ash trees growing just beyond the bridge float past them to jam against the stones of the opposite bank. It would be easy enough to wade across. The river does fill and darken in winter, turning brown and foamy as porter for a few days after every storm: though it takes a while – something up to twenty-four hours – for storm water from upstream in the rainy Corrèze to reach us. But most of the time this is a languid, easy stream.

Both the swimming hole and its pebble beach are remnants

of a village mill and ford. A tractor, or livestock, would still make easy work of this crossing, which everyone round here used until the Fifties, when the cement frame bridge was built a few hundred yards upstream. The mill is now a handsome, blue-shuttered holiday home, wisteria-clad and maintained year round by caretakers. Only a few dead leaves stir the surface of its swimming pool. Alas, the absentee English owners have told everyone to get off their land so often that most locals now do, although paths snake through the orchard fields. Since they don't maintain their stretch of river, parts of the crossing itself have become so silted up that they're like quicksand. The first time we sneaked across I lost a boot, and had to limp home stinking of waterweed.

But I'm dry-shod today as we stroll back up the grassy track. On our right are acres of sunflowers. Their blackened heads all hold the exact same angle between sun and earth as if, having stared the one in the eye and been blinded by it, they've assented to the pull of the other. Each tournesol is a mophead puppet, strung between these two poles of its being as between a pair of hands. The plants are surprisingly tall; taller than me at any rate. The dogs love threading beneath their canopy of leaves and seed-heads, where the trapped stink of field mice and rabbits must be almost overpowering. Zoi starts a strange, blood's-up yapping. Dusha trembles and rushes to and fro as if she were held on some short invisible lead.

The fields belong to Paulette's son Alain. We often see him at about this time, off to work on some outlying acreage. Two Alsatians ride his tractor pillion, balancing between axle and cab and barking so hard that we make bets on which will fall off first. Or they bound down in a topple of fur, a flash of tail held high. Then both dogs trot alongside the vehicle, barking at us as they pass. They scare Zoi in particular – her hackles snake along her back – because this isn't the gestural feinting of a collie running in circles, they don't have the high-pitched, keen-kid collie bark; bark but something altogether tougher and more gravel-voiced. Their trot, too, has aura of threatening capacity. It's a kind of pacing motion; they throw their front paws out ahead of their legs as if doing something so boring and easy they scarcely notice.

Alain has a herd of Limousin beef cattle; the calves are Paulette's special responsibility and joy. She refuses all evening invitations because she has to 'make sure they're settled for the night'. We've never seen these almost legendary beasts. They spend most of the year in a long, tin-roofed stone barn that stands perpendicular to her little chalet, dwarfing it and making it look more like a Wendy House than ever. The calves themselves keep surprisingly quiet. Only now, as we pass right by the barn's back wall, can we hear them shift and snort on the other side. It's a comfortable noise, one that sounds as though they're concentrating on a task they find not unpleasant. I say this to P, and he tells me, 'You'd concentrate, too, if you had to eat breakfast without using your hands.'

Back at the house, the dogs slurp down some water. Zoi kicks over a bowl in her excitement; it goes scattering and clanging across the tiles. P puts a thick log on the fire. I fill the coffee pot and set it to heat. We have a gas stove, and the pot balances awkwardly on the hob. When it starts bubbling the coffee that gurgles out of the spout will put out the flames, so I stand watch, inhaling the aroma of Sumatran beans. Not a bad life.

Eleven a.m. Through the open door of their back shed Nicolas and Jeannot can be seen – and heard – moving between huge wooden workbenches. Even in this confined space they're shouting at each other, though neither is angry. Shouting's just simply part of the working day, a sort of rhetoric of volume. Shouting indicates that the shouter is busy handling knowledge and responsibility: it also keeps the adrenaline going. Shouted abbreviations exclaim: This is no time for niceties!

Occitan helps this along. The somehow cursive quality it shares with Italian and Spanish is very different from the ordered, punctual character of French. *M'viste!* is so much quicker to yell than *Dépêche-toi.* First syllables, then consonants, drop away as father and son put distance between themselves and the farmstead. *M'vis... Vi...!* When the Savignacs cross the river and climb the wooded headland to the clearing where they grow their vines, language seems to drop away altogether. We encounter them there sometimes, driving the truck back down the steep hill to Exorbepay, a beefy forearm hanging symmetrically out of each front window. But if we try to hail them their responses are uncharacteristically vague.

Something determined and faraway creeps into their matching expressions out here on the limestone *causse.* (This name for the commonest of limestone formations comes from their own tongue: it's the Occitan for 'plateau'.) Seeing them up here where the Périgordian countryside rolls away for miles, its woods and farmland uninterrupted by urban sprawl, means seeing them both out of context and truly in it. This is deep France, *la France profonde.* Its history has been bloody yet something, some almost vegetal capacity for resurgence perhaps, asserts the continuity and vitality of a farming life that is simultaneously local and vast. You can see the old way of life going on for dozens and dozens of kilometres, ridge after sunlit ridge right to the horizon.

The Savignac vines keep company with a huge old fig tree. *Il en faut*, is all the reason for this that Jeannot can give. He doesn't like figs. He asks us to help ourselves, as the uneaten fruit simply attract wasps which make working among the vines unpleasant. But everyone who plants vines plants a fig, this familiar of the limestone landscape. *Il en faut.* And sure enough, there at the edge of the Savignac's hilltop plot is the branching, jaunty *Ficus carica*: dressed up in its smooth leaves and the light that scatters through them as if it counts itself in some way *comme il faut*.

But however much we covet them we can never quite bring ourselves to pick the fruit with their pinched purple necks, their grooved skins and bulgy, wine-bladder bodies. There's always just the faintest fear that we might have got someone else's field by mistake. For nothing here is hedged or fenced in, and there are no gates or signposts to identify the place as belonging to the Savignacs. Sometimes, we stumble upon a family parked up on the verge of a lane, working a patch of land they claim to be able to differentiate from other patchwork holdings mostly gone back to woodland. These visits of reclamation usually involve territorial strimming or scything. A complex picnic entailing a dozen or more Tupperware boxes waits on a rug. Canvas chairs have been placed along the grass. A couple of languidly fed-up teenagers lounge about. Often a small ill-mannered terrier barks from the back seat of the car.

For the most part though this high *causse* is strikingly depopulated. The old places strung along the ridge are a chain of saints' names: Saint-Michel, Saint-Raphael, Saint-Pantaly-d'Excedeuil, Saint-Martial-d'Albérède, Saint-Martin. On clear autumn days a vast light bleaches the limestone of old barns, abandoned cottages and road-corner Calvaries. If you were born here, wouldn't you think you were closer to the angels than the people who live down in the loamy river valley?

Today, when we sound the horn to see whether the Savignacs need anything from town, Jeannot waves from the shadows in the back of the shed and carries on working. But Nicolas, always eager for variety in the working day, comes to the door for a chat. Both men are wearing dramatically blood-stained white aprons, starburst splashes of vividly coloured fresh blood overlaying the darker, older patches. They look like Halloween costumes: it's hard to believe so much blood could be real, until Nicolas wipes a hand on his apron and I notice that its every cuticle and crease is bloodied red.

Behind him, standing at a bench, Jeannot handles the chopper. A pale mass of something falls open with a muted, chunking noise as the knife descends. *Thunk! Thunk!* goes his blade in the land where the guillotine was, incredibly, last used in 1977. You can see by the elbow action how satisfying it is to chop through the bird as though through a taboo; to split the bone and muscle and skin that was only just now alive. Exhilarating, too, the reality of your by now tremendous skill and speed: Jeannot, who must be in his middle sixties, has been doing this for half a century or more.

Watching him I can also see how, in butchering, you dominate the carcass and make it the raw material of your craft. It's pure will acting – *thunk, snicker-snick* – upon the world. And it is utterly different from the middle-class, conciliatory roles in which we busy ourselves proceeding according to the other guy: teaching, nursing, administering. Butchering, like much of farming, is an escape from the sheer frustration of dealing with people. Small wonder that the shouts we hear from the killing shed are the loudest of the week, and that both men emerge beaming after a session at the block.

Sure enough, they're grinning now. Jeannot's cheeks have taken on a high colour that matches the blood lying in gouts on the scarred wood of the workbench. Nicolas is breathing heavily through his nose as he stands talking. He has the air of a healthy young animal at its exercise. No thank you, they don't need anything from town: they'll be off there themselves soon. Behind him, the rhythm of chopping is broken by the sudden gush and roar of a tap being turned on. Water splashes up the walls and onto the floor, turning the concrete dark. *Nicolas!* Jeannot chides. Time to get back to work; to the messy, necessary business of sluicing down.

A dark tongue of water fringed with sawdust makes for my feet, and I retreat into the yard. The sunlight comes back as a surprise, reminding me how dark and cellar-like the interior of the shed is. I simulate being hurried away so that I won't have to kiss Nicolas. Quotidian Nicolas I have no objection to kissing three times in the local way, but bloodied Nicolas is a quite different matter.

In the car we fall to the enjoyable business of deciding what to get for lunch. No poultry, we agree, as P loads a CD of Terry Riley he knows I really hate into the car player. By the time we pull into the town square we're laughing so much that I can hardly breathe. We pretend this is about the

Riley, but we both know that really, we're children squealing with horror and relief at escaping from the killing shed.

And the square, of course, is a pleasure. We park between the huge lime trees that stand beside the river. Evidently someone had a recreation concession here once. Kayaks and canoes are alleged to frequent the Auvézère, though we've seen hardly a one. Still, here are the changing room and shower for river-muddied canoeists, and here a shuttered kiosk still lists the boating equipment it used to stock. There's a generous concrete launching ramp, and along the bank a set of municipal benches are going gradually adrift from their plinths.

Predictably, the square itself is gravelled. How does it manage to look so good? We never see it raked or replenished though I'm certain it must be once or twice a year at least. It's so absolutely not the unpaved 'Parking' of the Balkans, nor the broken-down British car park from which asphalt gradually takes its leave. Exactly done, from its pleached limes to its gravel, the *place* seems a satisfying triumph of will over matter. We can choose, it says, to be not slaves but masters of our circumstance.

I used to think there was a contradiction between Marianne, the Revolutionary Republican figurehead of France, and Napoleon, the self-crowned emperor who was allowed to arrogate that Revolution to himself. But don't you think, I say to P as we pocket our wallets and stroll to *La Poste*, that really it's the same impulse? The same notion that pure human will can and should rule? Napoleon merely took the notion to hubristic lengths. (At this point we go in and buy our stamps from Madame Dubois.) And isn't it interesting, I find myself resuming as we step out again, the doorbell chiming behind us, that the same impulse is at work in the traditional countryside *and* informing France's famous urban intelligentsia? The same belief in the conscious world, whether reason or will?

P agrees: after all, if you think about it they have a sort of Napoleonic Code in the kitchen. All this *comme il faut*. Madame La Poste is correct all day at work, then she goes home to be correct in the kitchen too. Well, not *all* day, he catches himself, and we start to laugh. We love our neighbours for their short working days and familial way of life – their two-hour lunch breaks, their afternoons off, the preponderance of public holidays – even though we feel guilty when we follow their model. But we're also inconsistent enough to be exasperated that we have to break off to shop *in the middle* of the working day.

The best things in the *boulangerie* are the *pain rustique*, which is made from a coarse, unbleached white flour, and the almond croissants, which aren't really croissants any more. Yesterday they were fresh-baked and springy, but this morning they've been flattened and refried in sweet almond dust. Butter leaks onto the pink paper bag that P carries them in, darkening it and turning it transparent as we stroll back towards the car.

The street is somnolent, warm, deserted. It offers us a quasi-mediaeval perspective, the houses with their tall Périgordian roofs standing around at angles to the road. The mediaeval limestone facades gleam palely, and shutters painted in white and faded blue lie back against them like the leaves of open books. A telephone wire hangs loosely across the street. Satellite dishes perch among the dormer windows; not even a pigeon stirs.

The little town of Tourtoirac isn't much more than a single street, though some houses straggle away from the main road that, lined with houses built between the fifteenth and nineteenth centuries, follows the river. The real reason for the settlement stands to our right behind a high buttressed wall. The road over the bridge mounts the little limestone ridge that the Auvézère delineates. It climbs to the hamlet of Beau-Site, then disappears into woodland; Excedeuil, administrative headquarters of the district, lies on the far side. But this shallow river, with its low banks, is conducive to easy crossing for many kilometres in both directions including, of course, at the ford in our own hamlet. What brought the crossing here in particular was the Abbaye St-Pierre-Ès-Liens.

The abbey was established by charter in 1025, by which time work on the building had already been underway for two decades. Its founders were Gui, Viscount of Limoges, and the Benedictine Abbot Etienne of Uzerche. They picked a good spot, on rich alluvial soil. What remains of the St-Pierre-Ès-Liens today is a tall nave church; high up in its shadows, the capitals of its long-legged pillars are stylised, chunky plants typical of the Romanesque. The best examples cluster behind the high altar in a dim apse, peeling and damp, that has the discouraging smell of uncared-for buildings.

You enter this apse from the other, north side of the church. There, protected by a further high wall, the fragmentary remains of the rest of the abbey stand among the gravel and lawn of a nineteenth-century *maison de maître*, now the home-cum-consulting rooms of an elderly doctor. There's a small chantry chapel, an abbot's kitchen, and the *salle des capitaux*, a long cellar enclosing an arcade on whose eponymous capitals tonsured, skirted men tug at each others' beards, and link arms in a dance. Does this beard tugging symbolise friendship or portray some other, more formalised, complicity? We're not able to guess, and the abbey's one-room museum offers no answers.

Still, the chunky, vivid carving of the figures is everything we love about the Romanesque, that architectural and artistic movement – from the eleventh and twelfth centuries in particular – that had its greatest flowering here in the south-west of France. In fact, our abbey is unusual in not being Cluniac. It was the Order's virtual monopoly on the Compostela pilgrimage routes that made them such great patrons of Romanesque art. As we drive back home, we speculate that perhaps Tourtoirac missed out because it lies so close to, yet not actually *on*, the Via Lemovicensis.

Back in the hamlet, Clarette's car is already parked outside her parents' house. She comes home for lunch every day, just as she must have all her life; although her own small, immaculate house is at the far end of Le Chambon. Sure enough, when P winds down his window, a garlicky scent of chicken broth is appetisingly in the air.

All of it again now, in reverse. Nicolas is waving at us once more; this time he stands apron-less at his front gate, waiting for Jazz to appear. Posed there with the range of barns and the farmhouse behind him, he looks like the farmer in a children's picture book. His mother's red geraniums are lined up in pots along the railings and on the tiled steps leading to her front door. They too seem like an illustration from a children's book. Everything down to the blue and yellow check curtains in the kitchen window is cheerfully, stoutly *comme il faut*. We round the corner and discover Jazz sniffing wistfully at our gate.

And so we arrive at the long lunch that shapes the provincial French day, and while everyone stops work a kind of silence falls in the village, though birds continue to quarrel in the poplars by the river. In the long sigh of noon contentment, we watch from our desks as our dogs stretch and turn on the warming stone flags of the yard.

After a while I have the idea of checking on our apricot tree. We planted the bare root sapling just last week; it stands at the end of a line of plum trees, looking as yet rather twiggy. The dogs accompany our inspection, although Zoi's on a warning. Last week she killed one of the Savignacs' chickens. There are always a couple of escapees fussing in the grass behind the sheds, and she had dragged one off behind a manure pile to feast on it: a useless subterfuge since we guessed the crime immediately. First her absence and then her guilty muzzle, sticky with blood and with a single downy feather riding on it, gave her away. As we also guessed, she couldn't resist going back to the corpse; we followed her and discovered the evidence. But when I confessed to Jeannot he simply laughed. She's new to it, he said, she'll learn. They kill one, or two, and then they learn. And Nicolas, coming up behind him grinning: Tie it round her neck for a day, she won't do it again. We don't share their confidence. But we're grateful for their generosity: after all the birds are the bulk of their livelihood. So we're eager for Zoi not to test such good neighbourliness, and we stop both dogs straying as far as the quince beside the poultry run.

The fruit on this gate-keeper are surprisingly dark skinned. It still surprises me, although it shouldn't, that even true quince, *Cydonia oblonga*, differ from each other just as apples do. Some varieties, Vranja for example, are almost lemony in colour. The bumpy flesh around the calyx at their base is pronounced, and their skin's shiny and clear. These are the Golden Delicious of quinces. Others such as Lusitanica have a mossy, green-gold skin that's almost scaly or hairy like a russet apple. I'm always surprised not to find the different varieties piled side by side on the fruit stalls in local markets, the way they are in the Balkans; but it seems that most Périgordian farmers are like the Savignacs. They don't treat quince as a commercial crop though they'll keep a single tree for family use.

Perhaps because they aren't generally hand fruit, but are served cooked, when I look at them I don't *see a taste*. This makes them seem arcane. Here in the hamlet Nanette and Francis – the Belgian couple who come and go every few months – also have a quince. They too leave their fruit on the tree as a kind of living larder. Quince, like game, must be hung to become tasty, the fruit bletted by first frost before it can be eaten raw. The Belgians' fruit are bright, canary-yellow globes on the almost bare November twigs. Those on the Savignacs' tree are drabber in appearance, but still sheltered by large, greenish leaves. I wonder whether we should grow a tree ourselves. Next to the apricot perhaps.

Three p.m. Time for the bonfire. Our gate swings open with its unoiled whinge, and Nicolas and Jazz appear in the kitchen. There's an outbreak of noise. Wild with joy, Jazz races upstairs to find our dogs, who greet him with yelps of enthusiasm. The pack comes skidding back downstairs and circles the kitchen table, yelling, till P manages to deflect them into the yard.

Meanwhile Nicolas, not a quiet talker at any time, is happily insisting on the bonfire essentials. We need matches, newspaper and not diesel, no – he shakes a broad finger – but something combustible. P returns. Nicolas tells him the same thing, regardless of the fact that P speaks neither French nor Occitan: matches, newspaper. But not diesel, no. He clicks his tongue, shaking his head. We feel as reproved as if the idea of using diesel had ever occurred to us. And as we follow him out into the brisk autumnal sunlight P and I exchange glances. The same thought is going through both our minds: surely he doesn't mean to use petrol instead?

Out in the orchard Jeannot is already at the unlit bonfire. Sometimes, in repose, the downward pull of his facial muscles gives him an expression of dismay, and he's looking dismayed right now. For a moment it seems as though we have committed some bonfire solecism.

Then he looks up and relieves us by smiling. At his feet is a huge tractor tyre. With gestures he indicates to P that he's rolled it himself from the Dutch barn where the harvester lives. Nicolas is delighted. The tyre will be sacrificed to make a real blaze. Thus is it confirmed to us that the problem with diesel is indeed one of safety, not ecological concern. We're dismayed; and at the same time an odd sensation of collusive glee rises in the pit of my stomach. I suspect it rises in P's too: I can tell he's trying not to catch my eye. As he approaches Jeannot, gesturing in turn his interrogation, I note the back of his neck is blushing, the way it does when something thrills him.

P and Nicolas bend with a kind of masculine tenderness to each side of the fire. Nicolas uses matches, which he crunches along the side of the matchbox, a man who doesn't know his own strength. He sets a fire again and again at the dry beech leaves. P has a lighter: he makes little feints here and there along the papery rim of the pile. Each time, the light curls briefly over his thumb. The catching flames are frail and blueish in the grey-blue shadowy pile of the bonfire. It seems impossible that they could be equal to it. Behind Nicolas his father grumbles: *Non, non, il faut…* But it's not clear what's necessary. Hitching his trousers, the older man strides off to a barn; he comes back with an armful of flattened cardboard boxes. Soon, they're on the pile and in flames. Soon too, the tyre follows as together father and son heft it onto the heap.

Now the acoustic of the fire is changed. It echoes inside the rubber ring. Then with equal abruptness a flame roars and the tyre is alight. A great plume of black smoke rises into the sky: above the trees, the telegraph poles, our house and barn. It seems to stream out of the pyre like something that merely needed to be released; a folding, flexible flow like the current of a river. At its foot, the fire is developing a neon-orange heart that silhouettes every stacked twig and branch, as if we should recognise and tally each one before it disappears in the flames. As a barely perceptible breeze of convection rises from the river, the plume balances and adjusts: it seems almost sentient in the subtlety of its reactions.

And now all the dogs of the hamlet have started barking. At first it's just Jazz running in wildly excited circles round and round the fire. He seems to be beside himself, yet all the time he gives it a wide, sagacious berth and keeps rolling his eyes towards the flames. Then Zoi and Dusha join in from our walled yard, yelping with pure frustration until we open the gate and let them come at a gallop into the orchard. Next Suzi storms up the lane and takes her stand at the boundary. Her furious warning barks are spaced with pauses, her tone is admonitory and her hackles are up. And now from beyond the high roof of our house comes the booming note of the Belgians' moon-gold retriever Debussy, and then, a little further off, Alain's Alsatians. Even the woodsman's Doberman across the river rattles his chain and starts to roar.

Now Madame Savignac herself comes slowly out of the house to watch. She moves as if her body were a dangerous object that must be handled gently. And so it must. She's just back from a month in hospital in Périgueux, where she was rushed with an embolism. She is a big woman and her body encloses her like a trap. She's clearly terrified of having another clot. She often finds it difficult to breathe, and every time she does so I worry for her. As she walks she gasps, and levers her weight painstakingly from leg to leg.

It's a cruelty that long understanding of how to live well should today threaten Madame Savignac's life. She's the kind of gifted household manager whose tremendous will comes out in the volume of her voice, but is concealed by the quick, easy movements of her craftswoman's hands. Madame Savignac – *But you must call me Françoise,* she urges – is a wonderful cook. All their life she's fed her family foie gras and roasted goose, potatoes cooked in lard and cheeses thick with cream, *tartines* made with buttery pastry, doorsteps of bread spread thickly with butter, breakfast bowls of hot chocolate, *sirops* of blackcurrant and even of walnut, and huge stews garlanded with dumplings.

Such cooking is a celebration of life. Whatever can be eaten should be enjoyed, is the logic of her farm kitchen. And so her days and months move not with a crushing, parsimonious sense of routine but, in constant anticipation, from pleasure to pleasure. For after the strawberries there are currants, the red and the black; and after the cherries come greengages, and after the greengages are red and purple plums, and they are followed by apples and *tarte Tatin*, the upside-down pudding that the region claims as a speciality. And so it goes. This week she will at last make the thick quince jelly that goes so well with the local cheeses. The sour soft goats' cheese of *Cabécou du Périgord* (its name from *cábro*, the Occitan for goat), and *Crottin de Chavignol*, go especially well with quince, whether jellied or baked. At this time of year the fruit also makes frequent appearances at her table baked with honey and walnuts. Its flesh is rich and almost treacly – though the cooked skin has a tendency to get between the teeth.

Françoise also loves the outdoor life of the farm. Sometimes she sits on the front wall, knitting and talking, with Paulette or Marie. Equally often, we pass and find the friends paused in companionable silence which they interrupt to wave a greeting or call a question. They must have sat like this together through the decades, growing from young to middle-aged women, and then by slow degrees becoming old: although Paulette and Marie are each a good decade senior to Françoise, who sometimes nowadays sits here with little Josette instead. Her granddaughter fidgets with her knitting wool as small girls will; or else she runs off into the yard to play with Jazz.

Young Josette loves Jazz, and he loves her. When they're together he's constantly coaching her to play, nudging her with his muzzle or gently butting her legs to make her run. He prances round her as he does round Nicolas and, like Nicolas, she responds to this ring-dance of adoration by laughing and calling his name, *Jazz, Jazz!* Josette is a little scrap of a thing, pale-faced and with pale blonde hair. She makes an odd contrast to her monumental grandmother, whose hair is dyed the dark colour of the south. It seems impossible that Josette, still almost disappearingly shy, could grow up to be as tough and certain as her grandmother or indeed her mother; but perhaps this kind of strength remains dormant in early life. We take extrovert children to be the strongest characters. But how might a slower-fused, quiet certainty show itself during childhood?

Clarette and her mother have the air of having been born wise. Though nothing they say is particularly vatic, I always have a sense of their exceptionally strong personal compasses. You couldn't make either of them do something they believed was wrong, whether immoral or impractical. From her post at the *Mairie*, Clarette effectively runs the little town of Tourtoirac, and she does so with a steady, unswerving hand. In the clattering, tiled depths of her farmhouse kitchen Madame Savignac steers her family and their farm with equal confidence.

Perhaps little Josette's silence is a sign that she's inherited these qualities; maybe she doesn't need to show off to us. Or perhaps she's simply silent because the rest of the family make so much noise. Swinging on a chair back, she hums faintly to herself. Sitting on her mother's knee she'll turn and hide her face when her uncle Nicolas or her grandfather Jeannot speaks to her. Yet she follows both these larger-than-life characters everywhere around the farm. Both clearly dote on her too, and they let her follow like a mascot wherever the work isn't too dangerous. She watches as they clean the tractor, or unclip its flanks to work on the engine. She accompanies them to the poultry run when they collect the eggs. She hops among the fallen leaves of the sweet chestnut while they argue.

Just now she's following her grandmother instead. She waits with grandmaman at the yard railing and together they watch the bonfire as it begins to die down. The men are disappointed about this but its work is done. The fire-worshipper in each of us flickers and must go out. Besides, the afternoon is wearing on. The Savignacs' working day ends at around five in time for an *apéro*. Soon Clarette will be dropping by the farm to pick up Josette and give her mother a summary of the afternoon's news from Tourtoirac. Only on special occasions – and every Wednesday and Friday – does she stay for a drink to mark the day's end. On these evenings Josette gets to play late with Jazz, to repeat her counting skills to her grandpère, and to take a tiny Josette-sized sip of *bernache* from her mother's glass.

We can't help feeling that the orchard is more the Savignacs' back yard than it is ours. They've earned their place in this landscape by knowing how to farm it. Provident, canny, never unaware, they're our hosts here and we are grateful to them. We thank them again, wave to Josette, kiss Madame. But five o'clock is too early for us to stop for the day. Back in the house, I put more coffee on the stove. We shrug into sweaters and coats. We'll take our work out on the back stoop until it's dark.

The outdoor light is starting to change, though not yet to dim. The smell of the bonfire, acrid with burnt rubber, floats faintly on the air. It's joined now by the sweeter smell of wood smoke as the *cheminées* of the hamlet begin to light. A thin line of white smoke from Michel and Marie's farm rises above the roof of our barn. It bends neither right nor left till it gets above the trees, where it bunches and dissolves in the open air. After a while Michel himself appears, passing up the track. He's followed by Suzi, who rests her black muzzle between the bars of our gate to gaze in angrily. On the stoop beside us Dusha raises her head, then relaxes with a dismissive grunt.

Michel pauses to inspect the remains of the bonfire. *Bonne idée*, he congratulates us. The fire puffs gently. Something rolls apart. A bright ember is briefly visible, a piece of charred wood crackles. After an awkward moment I put down my work to go and stand beside him. Together we watch the busy, patchy work of fire among the embers. It looks satisfyingly as though there will be nothing left tomorrow but ash.

Yesterday was All Saints' Day, La Toussaint, and almost everybody in the village went to visit their family graves. It's hard not to think about this, or to have the sense of a changeover between the generations, between cultures, as we regard the autumn bonfire. But Michel is far too private a man for me to refer to anything like this. And maybe that costive, wry expression just means he's contemplating the mysteries of indigestion.

Yesterday afternoon a strange silence fell in the hamlet; a drowsy sense of the exceptional. Work stopped on all the holdings: on Michel's land down by the river, at Paulette's house and in the cowshed, on her son's fields, and everywhere on the Savignacs' farm. The electric saw, so often droning at the woodsman's house on the other side of the river, fell silent. There was a sense of purposeful waiting. In the shuttered hallways of the houses flower arrangements, many of them plastic, waited on hall tables. Here and there a car door slammed, an engine started up, as families set off to visit graves left behind in distant cemeteries. The Savignacs bundled into their old Peugeot estate – a surprising vehicle, brought out only on special occasions – for once without a wave. Left behind, even the dogs fell silent, drowsing in their winter quarters.

On this morning's trip to town we saw the resulting cacophony of plastic blooms on local graves. Tourtoirac's *cimetière* is walled in the French way, as if to keep the dead safely corralled. Hard to think of being buried there as being 'laid to rest': the place seems to be all unyielding stone and concrete. Gravel paths run between headstones set into cement plots. Here and there a vast limestone slab roofs a family vault, but elsewhere it's hard to understand how the citizens of Tourtoirac even *get* interred.

We don't visit graveyards at this time of year: that would be an intrusion. But we've often walked round them together. It's perhaps here that I feel most foreign in Périgord. There's a relentlessness, an in-your-face built-ness, to these systematic sites. Their very lack of any suggestion of corporeal rest is meant, of course, to suggest that these are mere memorials: the dead are 'resting' not here, but 'with God'. All the same, you can't help feeling that French graves tend to be arranged on a panopticon principle: all must be equally seen, and seen to be equal. There's none of the nostalgia for the land that keeps even city graveyards in Britain edged with grass and planted with flowers.

Suzi gives up on Dusha in disgust, shakes herself, and comes to stand by Michel. Her master clicks his tongue to her, smiles goodbye, and moves slowly away down the track. I have, as usual, no idea what he's thinking. I look back at our house, silhouetted against the sky. On the first-floor stoop, P's laptop screen is an incongruous pane of blue light, but there are shadows round his feet and under his chair, and the half-open doorway behind him is completely dark. As I climb the steps to join him, he looks up in surprise: his eyes are completely attuned to the bright screen. He blinks and rubs them as I sit down beside him to watch the sky change.

Now the evocative shapes of the roofs come into their own. In Périgord most hamlet's are darkly clay-tiled, and contrast with the pale stone of the house walls: strangely, the tradition here is not for split stone slates as it is in English limestone areas. Gables are sharply peaked and form a concave angle that works the opposite way from the convex elbow-joints of mansard roofs. High and steep, Périgordian roofs flare outward at their midpoint. By French standards they have to shrug off a lot of rain, and they're designed to slice narrowly upward, offering a minimal surface area and nowhere for water to pool.

Above this characteristic roofline the westerly sky is growing pale. It's still – just – blue, but the blue is fringed now with peach. The old house wall is cooling. I lean against it, feeling the roughness of undressed stone. Between the trees a mist is rising from the river. Trunks of ash and wild cherry march darkly through it, as if towards us. On the far bank, where the woods crowd down to the river, chestnut and sycamore are slowly losing themselves in the dusk.

It's time to take the dogs for their evening walk. We get up and they're at our heels, all alacrity. Dusha bounds and barks: it seems she's not, after all, the most depressed dog in the world. Zoi starts pawing my thigh, as if that will persuade me to move quicker. And so with much skittering excitement we're off, this time to cross the river and make the loop along the opposite bank.

We pause at the bridge. Evening has turned the water

brown. The shadows of the trees that flank it make pools of deeper black in the dark water. Small wonder the river boasts good trout and carp fishing. It has gravelly pools and, in the rich vegetal muck that collects at the banks, a vigorous insect life. (One great blessing of the frosts of the last week has been that, at last, the mosquitos have disappeared.)

Like all the rivers of Périgord Vert, the Auvézère is a very *manageable* waterway. The Vézère, which here runs roughly parallel to our river and around twenty kilometres to the south, is fundamentally similar but larger. It too flanks limestone bluffs from which a fertile riverside can be observed, laid out invitingly downstream or on the opposite bank. The natural shelter of cliffs and caves, accessible water, an easy terrain rich in plant and animal life: these landscape elements coincided to enable unsheltered humans' earliest settlement of the cool, damp European continent. It's fewer than twenty-five kilometres from here to the Vézère valley near Montignac, where the 19,000-year-old cave paintings of Lascaux and beyond wait, sealed now but still extraordinary, for posterity.

As we take the path along the Auvézère's further bank we pass under wild chestnut and cherry, oak and birch. This mixture is characteristic of wild seeding yet the trees are generously spaced, with little or no self-seeded brash clotting the ground beneath them. The woods are primeval in the sense of being unplanted, but they've been loosely managed for centuries: used to graze pigs and to hunt deer and rabbits, coppiced and sometimes stripped for firewood and building timbers. Not here, but in the less frequented woodland further uphill, the black truffles on which the region prides itself can also be found.

Paulette boasts that her son Alain is the best truffle-hunter in the village. Fruit of rot, the black-spored root *Tuber melanosporum* loves damp, alkaline limestone soil. The black clayey fungi grow below ground, like bulbs, under the oak trees of scrubland and woods. Many *caveurs* use dogs to sniff them out. But Alain's Alsatians, impatient and extrovert, are the wrong temperament for truffle hounds. Instead he uses his own senses to detect the tangy, secretive odour of *truffes* among woodland smells that rise strongly in the riverine air of autumn evenings like this. I don't enjoy the clinging, slightly nauseating flavour of the delicacy as much as I should, but P does. So do our neighbours, who grate and slice crumbs of truffle into their favourite dishes, omelettes and pâtés, and will, on special occasions, bake whole *truffes en croûte* with a smear of foie gras and a slice of air-dried ham.

The woods are quite dark now, but full of noises. Branches crack as the trees cool and settle for the night, and birds call their fractious evening chorus. Yet the river to our right seems glassily still. Only occasionally an insect, catching the skim like a pilcrow, highlights itself with concentric ripples that scatter the light. And once or twice a roach or bream, jumping for the last insects of the day, breaks the surface with a swallowing sound.

Now the embanked path turns away from the river to loop around the wood. We are in effect walking along a limestone wall, which must have been raised in mediaeval times when these fields were water meadows. Today they flood only in once-in-a-decade emergency. Indeed, the turreted *manoir* of La Farge, there on the other bank, stands so close to the water in which it's reflected – a blocky mass

– that the Auvézère must have stopped flooding regularly by the sixteenth century when it was built.

At the time, Périgord was celebrating its emergence from the Hundred Years' War. That bitter religious and territorial conflict, fought between England and France from 1337 to 1453, devastated a region that was still reeling from earlier depredations. Famines had recurred since 1310; the Black Death, which reappeared in the south of France in 1348, went on to kill between one-fifth and one-third of the country's entire population. All of which horror is recorded and transformed by Périgord's remarkably homogenous vernacular architecture, the joyously tall-roofed, high-walled villages and towns into which the local limestone flowered between the late fifteenth and the seventeenth centuries.

At the end of the embankment our path enters a farmyard built in just this style. It stands closed up all year round. This evening the apple trees in its abandoned orchard are still starred with fruit, and dew has turned the giant cobwebs that deck them gauzy. It's with some difficulty that we call the dogs away from ratting round the locked-up barns and on through the walnut orchards that line the road here.

The raked grass between the trees shows bleached in the half-light. Their serrated leaves are golden and red-brown. As we pass more float down. The air's full of woodsmoke, but also of the tea-leaf odour of autumn leaves. Both smells hang in the dampness with which the air, I suddenly notice with a shiver, seems impregnated.

Acre after acre the orchards of *noyer* climb the slopes above us to open into high grazing at the narrow top of the *causse*, where the few remaining family farms overlook vistas that open almost to the Auvergne. This evening those blue vistas tremble in our imaginations like so many flames.

Now even the closest trees are misty and blue. The pixelated dusk closes round us as we come into Exorbepay, the village on a bluff above the river. Our footsteps echo between the cottages smart with verandas and roof-lights. Many belong to a Dutch community of expat and holiday-home owners, who rake the bright-yellow gravel outside their model hay barns and *pigeonniers* with stringency. It seems nothing here could ever be out of place. The potted geraniums on the *grenier* steps have been positioned by design rather than ending up there by accident. The huge stones of walnut presses are fetishes for front yards. In rooms where the lights are already on, we see none of the messy, oil-clothed convenience of our neighbours' kitchens. A single bowl sits solemnly on a polished wooden table. A spray of lavender, tied with a pale-blue ribbon, hangs from a beam above a nineteenth-century buffet.

Although the lights are on, the village is entirely silent. It feels slightly suffocating, ghostlier even than the abandoned houses that we come across sometimes, slipping back into the landscape under festoons of old man's beard and bramble. They at least seem to belong in the same world as the woods and fields that surround them; to be made of the same materials, limestone and clay. And indeed they are as much part of the Périgordian farming life as its orchards, fields and hunting woodland. French inheritance laws mean that children have automatic, and inalienable, inheritance rights. It only needs one sibling to refuse to cooperate, and a small family *ferme* can sit forever unsold and uninhabited.

Limestone has never seemed so friable as when these disputed houses begin to slide apart. First an ash sapling in the tiles, then tufts of couch grass hanging from the guttering, and very soon the roof is open to the weather. Once that happens the house walls, unprotected inside as out, become roosts for pigeons, bats and the barn owls we hear nightly calling from across the river.

Rats and foxes find their ways in too, but – a phenomenon that seems at first curious, then normal – here no one squats an abandoned house. The depopulated countryside is undergoing the opposite of a housing crisis: it even welcomes holidaying incomers and second-home owners because of the money and work they bring with them. Yet such incomers change the very thing they come for. However much they seem to admire Périgordian traditions, it's a largely cosmetic admiration. They like the rural artefacts – oil presses and hand ploughs – that they clean and preserve; but they don't try to make a living from the land.

In the museum silence of Exorbepay, the *clickety-click* of our dogs' claws is annoyingly audible. It reminds us we need to clip them, a job involving many pairs of gloves and muzzling blankets. But the whole thing's such a *hassle*, I grumble to P. He agrees: Let's not do it tonight.

We emerge from the village where the road makes an expansive circuit round a limestone basin. It's a lovely fluent shape, almost calligraphic in character. In karstology such closed limestone depressions, not fed or drained by rivers and springs, are usually called *polje*: from the Slav for 'field'. Such a delightful, rolling word, which I enjoy repeating – *polje, polje, polje* – until P loses patience, Enough with the Pollys!

Besides – he reminds me – as so often in limestone landscapes these bold, fluent lines aren't the full story. There's inconsistency and uncertainty here too, in the form of caves hidden below these rolling slopes. The Grotte de Tourtoirac, discovered in 1995 and opened to the public only in 2010, was found by potholers exploring the *guier*, or rise-pit, of a spring that used to be the town's main water supply. The rise-pit had in effect been disguised by its use as a *fontaine*, one of the traditionally roofed, open-air shelters at communal washing and laundry springs that used to serve the towns and villages of Périgord.

The discovery of the caves was a good news story for a district with very little employment beyond farming, where tourism has been too haphazard – or absent – to provide people with livelihoods. But as if chthonic forces really do live in such places, their exploration demanded its sacrifice. Jean-Luc Siriex, who discovered the caves on January 28 1995, drowned in them just one week later when he returned to explore further with three colleagues, one of whom was also killed.

Today the caves lie below a smart modern facility, and visitors are treated to an 'artistic' lighting display as well as the expertise of guides. P and I found the *son et lumière*, with its reliance on electro-drumming and its disco glows of pink, blue and green, simultaneously hilarious and frustrating. Such exquisite technological implementation could have been put to much better use; on our tour we became the bad children sniggering at the back of class.

But the caves themselves are spectacular in the usual way of caves, and they're Clarette's pride and joy, the chief treasure for which she's responsible at the *Mairie*. Above the buffet in the Savignac farmhouse hang framed photos of her and Nicolas wearing hard hats and yellow oilskins, and harnessed up to preview the complex. The family scrapbook is stuffed with cuttings in which – photographed sometimes bare-headed, sometimes in the hard hat – Clarette gets to represent the not-yet-opened cave complex, a newsworthy phenomenon in this quietest of neighbourhoods.

That quiet closes around us as we make our way back to the bridge. *Réserve de chasse*, says a sign on our right, white and conspicuous in the gathering dark. A repudiating bullet-hole punctures its tin. The dogs would like to disrespect the nature reserve too, but we have them on short leads. It feels as though the dusk is teeming with wild creatures – deer, boar, rabbits and foxes, rats and stoats – all of them waiting for us to leave. Twigs crackle surprisingly close by. Something takes a punt, races through the long grass and nettles, and drops into the river with a *plash*.

As we cross the river we feel cold air rising from the water. It's cooler still as we cross the last field to the hamlet. Night draws moisture up from the soil and out of the dead sunflowers to make a chill blanket of mist that grips our ankles and hurries us along the track. Even the dogs have their muzzles down and seem set for home. We swing the gate closed behind us with relief, and plunge into the brightness of the lamp-lit kitchen.

P is just unlacing his boots when we hear something strange outside. At first I can't make sense of it at all. Nor can the dogs. They freeze, staring up at the kitchen window. P pauses too. The noise seems not to come from any one direction but instead to surround the house. Even to call it 'noise' feels not quite right: it doesn't have, so to speak, discrete edges. It is, rather, a *state of* noise; something like air pressure. Still it's getting louder and closer. The air vibrates. And now this airy teeming begins to make sense, resolving itself into a carpet of cries, into the creaking, swiping sound of wing beats. It's clearly the sound of birds.

We hurry to the door. Outside, the sky is a clear and luminous blue but we can see nothing in it. And then we do. Very high up, in a streaming V formation, the great birds come flying from the east. Their loose-jointed flight looks graceful, effortless. They are migrating cranes following the Auvézère south and west towards Spain for the winter. Their rhythmic wing beat is strong and steady, strong and steady and it has lifted and carried them in a great arc all the way across Europe from Russia, Siberia, the Baltic.

Now the line breaks, and another V forms. Like the first, it is hundreds of birds long. The flock will surely pause soon for the night, landing somewhere downriver among the Auvézère's well-stocked shallows. I'd love to know where. The common crane, the *grue cendrée*, is neither common nor ashy, but as beautiful on ground as it is in the air. On land and water, even in the dark, it becomes a red-billed dancer with pluming tail. Meanwhile though, the twittering purring call continues all around us, wave after wave, until at last the final birds have passed overhead. And still it remains for some whole minutes, seeming to open in the space behind the flock like a wake.

At last the sky falls silent. The day is over. The Belgians have closed their shutters for the night. Only chinks of yellow light appear here and there among the darkly silhouetted buildings and trees of the hamlet. The Savignacs' yard is deserted. We go back inside, and P sets to stoking our *cheminée* with old oak planks. It roars in appreciation. The dogs shake themselves and settle in front of the blaze.

P goes round the house closing the shutters. I hear a

squeak of hinges, then the clunk of wood against frame. The sound repeats itself as he moves from room to room. Picking up a towel I open the oven door. Chicken juices crackle in the baking tray. The twigs of rosemary have gone black, but their aroma fills the kitchen. I drop the slices of steamed marrow into the chicken fat, and count on ten minutes to supper.

When I turn round, P is opening the wine. The smell of fresh air has caught in his clothes, a mnemonic of the November day. I light the candles, find some plates, sit down at table. He raises his glass. *Santat!*

Summer
Škocjan

Na zdravje!

I don't have a penknife but you produce a knife from your jacket pocket and cut through the wax seal round the bottle neck. You draw out the cork. It comes slowly, slowly. Then there's a pop and you pass me the opened bottle. I sniff it gingerly. The vapours sting my nose like smoke and condense at the rim of the bottle, frosting the glass.

'Try it,' you urge me, nodding and smiling. You put the brace of glasses down on the table between us. I pour: a single measure for myself, a double for you. You lift your glass in a toast, and I raise mine in answer. We each take a sip, your smile widens and I burst out laughing. This is *really* good slivovitz.

Twice-distilled plum brandy *sounds* as though it should be heady and sticky. But slivovitz is a clean spirit. Though it can certainly give the regular drinker an ulcer, he won't get many hangovers along the way unless he abuses it badly. Which is easy to do. Slivovitz is modest in its self-presentation, clear and colourless like vodka or gin. Unlike those other spirits, it's served in pinch-waisted sherry glasses up and down the Balkans, ubiquitous at formal occasions and parties, in bars and during lunches. The bottle we've just opened, for example, was made commercially, but by hand. It's expensive, fragrant, and strong enough to take our breath away. Clearly not the homemade stuff, so much more than 140 per cent proof, that gets produced in private, often illegal, stills in sheds and gardens across the region. Alcohol that's gone beyond mere liquor, this amateur slivovitz is so dangerous that to taste it can no longer be called taking a drink. It's like drinking meths, or battery acid.

What we're sampling now, on the other hand, sends a glowing, pleasurable ribbon along the tongue and down the throat. Plum, quince, grape; thyme and apple; hot earth, sunlight and a mountain wind. What would you get if you concentrated and attenuated all these ingredients – distilled them in fact?

If whisky should be cut with water, slivovitz should be cut with air. When we taste it sip by sip each of these flavours seems momentarily present. But slivovitz *is* twice-distilled and, as we swallow, the mineral note of alcohol carries everything else away. Flavours and memories: all disappear together with the shock of it. We blink and gasp, refill and clink our glasses. *Na zdravje*, you say. To health!

Elegies and Ballads

The bora has opened a window.
Hot stars
fall on the fields.

Srečko Kosovel

This is a story about the former Yugoslavia, and about how sometimes it becomes necessary to visit a place only after you've fallen in love with it. Or maybe it's about how narrow the gap is between people we love and the places where we love them. Or else this story is about how ideas and dreams, stories and proverbs, create the places that mean something to us. It's certainly the story of how a particular place is highlighted and shadowed by death – in the way it's been portrayed by writers down the years – the high, half-forgotten limestone country that the tragic Slovenian poet Srečko Kosovel made his own a hundred years ago.

To begin with though, it was just a dream of the good life. My lover S was Macedonian but I worked in London, and we used to fantasise about ways to stay together. Lying awake among the dark-wood fittings of post-communist hotel bedrooms, we planned that we would spend part of every year in Slovenia. We'd wander the mediaeval lanes of the old town of Piran and eat seafood in its harbour-front restaurants. We'd rent rooms cheaply out of season and write side by side in the languages we didn't have in common.

Piran, teetering along its promontory on the forty-seven-kilometre Adriatic coast of Slovenia, seemed to mark the exact midpoint between our lives, if not in time and space then culturally at least. Just as the former Yugoslavia had believed itself to be nonaligned during the Cold War, now the little country of Slovenia, snapped off from its top left-hand corner and one of the few areas to escape disaster as war broke up that state, seemed to have managed not to be quite in line with either the Balkan South or the Anglo-Americanised North.

When it came to it though, my first visits to the limestone Karst region that lies behind Piran – the 6,880 square kilometres that comprise western Slovenia – were made without S. And once we did meet there, nothing was as simple as we'd imagined. In Slovenia, S had always spoken the *lingua franca* of former Yugoslavia, which now goes by several names – Serbian and Croatian among them. It was the national language of the state he'd shared with Slovenes: a united country in which he could move freely and which he was part of. But in independent Slovenia Serbo-Croat had become, retrospectively, a colonising force. The small, newly confident Central European country, busy with its economic miracle, was in the business of refusing everything it saw as post-colonial. The old regional language was dismissed as Yugo-nostalgia at best, Serbian nationalism at worst.

On the main road west from Ljubljana we saw the evidence of this new national confidence. Those gleaming white blocks abutting the slip roads were factories and hypermarkets. Among the orchards of Ljubljansko Barje we recognised the Gorenje factory, now producing designer white goods for European luxury kitchens. Further out, the giant blue sign of a superstore above a warehouse. Below St Katherine's Hill, where our publisher friends Primož and Stanka lived with Primož's father in suburbia – roses and the family vine in the front garden – we saw the spreading gentrification prosperity brings to a small country whose citizens start from a position of broad equality. Broad-beamed SUVs were everywhere, parked beside sun terraces they towered over. Mobile-phone masts and advertising hoardings dotted the maize fields in this bowl of fertile soil between the hills, former marshlands that give Ljubljanans their nickname of *žaba*, or frog.

When Slovenia joined the EU in 2004, as one among the first tranche of post-communist 'accession countries', it joined the Schengen Area of free movement too. Now it became hard for S, as a citizen of excluded, chaotic Macedonia, to get the kind of visa that allows you to make extended visits to a country, leave alone to plan a life. And anyway there were things about Slovenia that I was finding hard to accept. One of these was a nationalism that seemed to have attained respectability in both its public and its intellectual discourses.

Small countries appear to find it easier to get away, morally as well as practically, with such rhetoric. They tend to have form as the periodic victims of mightier neighbours: Slovenia, like all the countries that once made up Yugoslavia, has long been squeezed between two empires, the Austro-Hungarian and the Ottoman. Nationalism then becomes a compensatory narrative, the dream that history will not repeat itself.

But the rudeness S met with as we moved west was more

complicated than this. That bus driver in Divača who refused to let us board when we didn't have the exact change. The woman in the bar in Koper who wouldn't serve us lunch, though she brought menus for the locals. S is no coloniser: no more a native speaker of Serbo–Croat than any Slovenian. The Macedonian language is closer to Bulgarian than it is to Serbian, and the accent is unmissable. It's thick and southern, clotted with sounds that more northerly Slavs mock as peasant speech. And so there it is: the usual north/south thing. S is as brown as his combined Greek, Turkish and Jewish ancestry can make him. Slovenians, who may tend to blond as children and turn ruddy in middle age, often resemble nothing so much as Bavarians. To be a Macedonian in Slovenia, we were discovering, was almost as bad as being one in Heidelberg, where we'd once spent a strange week living off junk food and walking a wintry Philosophenweg.

Slovenians excuse themselves for this kind of prejudice by saying that they're afraid of Serbia. On a September evening outside a bar on Rimska Cesta, Roman Road, in Ljubljana, nervy, smart Ana bends our ear. 'Have you any idea', she asks, 'what it was like when the Serbs sent their tanks in?' As if to prove her point that this is a Central European country which shouldn't be judged by Balkan standards, Ana is drinking not wine or slivovitz but Slovenian Laško beer, and its trademark Zlatorog, the golden-horned antelope, stares at us haughtily from the laurel wreath on the bottle. The sides of her glass are clouded by bubbles. The table is speckled with lime seeds and cigarette ash. 'They came within thirteen kilometres – *thirteen*. I mean, basically, they came right up to the city itself.'

We shake our heads in unison; I because I have absolutely no realistic notion of being in a war zone, S because his country is still at war. We all know the end of the story. Eighteen Slovenians, twelve foreign civilians, and an alleged forty-four Yugoslav army personnel were killed in the Ten Day War. In the event Ljubljana was unscathed. Indeed, of the former Yugoslav capitals, only Sarajevo became an actual battleground during the bloody wars of the Nineties: though what happened to that city was a terrifying warning to the rest, as the competing warlords intended.

Slovenia's gamble paid off. You might have said, as a contemporary Western onlooker, that this small country's declaration of independence from the rest of Yugoslavia, after the death of General Tito in Ljubljana in 1988 and the fall of the Berlin Wall in 1989, started the unravelling that accelerated into the Balkan tragedy. Once any one of the Yugoslav countries achieved independence others would want the same; and Belgrade would then have no option but either to use force, or else settle for becoming a rump Serbian state. (In the event it managed to combine both of those alternatives in the worst possible way.) But anyone who's spent time in the Balkans, or read even the most cursory account of their history, will tell you that the fault lines along which the region breaks and breaks again have existed since at least mediaeval times. They're the borders between religions – of not only the primary contest between Christianity and Islam but also of those defining internecine struggles within Christianity: between Rome and the old Holy Roman Empire, Catholicism and Orthodox Christianity – and between the western and southern empires, the Austro-Hungarian and the Ottoman, and their competing cultural legacies. Slovenia itself is a Catholic country whose capital is a conspicuously Austro-Hungarian architectural gem. Even this bar on Rimska Cesta is a brightly stuccoed eighteenth-century building, its characteristic machicolations and embrasures highlighted in two tones of yellow.

S reaches for Ana's lighter, a deliberative gesture that means he wants to change the subject. Ana doesn't notice. She rattles on, full of a self-absorption that I instantly identify as Western. Traces of the old socialist neighbourliness – still marked in these post-communist regions, though whether it was born of idealism or of hard times I'm never sure – survive in the Slovenian countryside; but here in town it's already hard to imagine there ever was a collective sensibility.

Ana finishes her beer and looks around for a waiter. 'I mean, I've nothing against Serbs,' she says. 'Except that they terrify me.' The waiter catches her eye and raises his fingers: One? Three? One, Ana gestures. S contemplates his coffee grounds glumly. He can't afford to buy a round himself, and he hates this kind of talk because for a Macedonian it's not abstract bar-room chatter but lived reality. News of the Tetovo Offensive is being broadcast night and morning from his home city of Skopje. The Macedonian capital, in its basin overlooked by high limestone mountains, is now only around forty kilometres from the Front. Every day, for the last few months, he and his daughters have heard the sound of the heavy artillery from the hills above them; every day the city that is their home has felt itself slipping closer and closer to sharing Sarajevo's fate. As Srečko Kosovel wrote after the First World War:

> People are like
> sinking, dimming lamps.

One unlikely courtesy that persists here is that you don't speak about what you really fear. So when the waiter arrives we make our escape. 'Well! Thank you for your company and the so-nice coffee,' S smiles, finding his purse. I watch helplessly as he counts out the money he's saved for his trip home. In just the last hour his face seems to have turned sallow, and filled with expressionist shadows.

All the same, our dream of Slovenia persists: and it is a dream of the Slovenian Karst land. One-third of the national territory is limestone country, after all. In this dream it's always August, with the dreamy sense of possibility Srečko Kosovel evokes in his poem 'Večerni hlad':

> Evening cool
> and the breeze beyond the garden –
> there, there the gleaming castle
> and there the open door

Late in another August, S and I are walking the little roads of the Lipizzaner stud farm near Sežana, in the western, Karst region of the country. Everywhere, white rail fences enclose pastures studded with orchard trees. It's a child's picture-book idea of countryside. In the paddocks, white *Lipicánec* horses move languidly among oak and apple trees. They're uninterested in visitors, having seen too many. This lack of interest combines with their ghostly colouring to give them an air of mystery; somehow, it seems as if they wear their own symbolic nature more than other horses do. It's easy to see why they've been so carefully treasured and bred through the centuries since they first found favour with the Hapsburg monarchy, who founded this stud in 1580. It's true that Lipizzaners are unusually agile and strong – just what a militarised monarchy needs – but they also *look* like lucky beasts; ensign and talisman together.

All the same, there are few visitors here today. Those who come mostly stay in a hotel at the centre of the farm complex: it's a remnant of centrally planned, Yugoslav-era tourism. Coaches sweep these residents off on trips. Now, in the hour before they return and after the day-trippers have left, the site is largely deserted. In this sunlit moment before dinner we have its acres to ourselves. An evening stillness settles. A horse snorts a couple of paddocks over. A trio of mares trot to the rail to greet us, heads back, stepping high. Even off duty, they act the way they have for more than four centuries in the sandy arena of the Spanish Riding School in Vienna. Is this just how they move? Or has some equine flirtatiousness been bred into them: are they showing off for us?

Other beasts, standing around in the middle distance, could be statues cut from the white limestone that lies just below the close-cropped turf. Occasionally this rock surfaces as erratic boulders, left here and there by retreating glaciers at the end of the last Ice Age, roughly 12,000 years ago. Lichen dapples these boulders, its punctuating circles a kind of ecological macramé. The grey dapples on the backs of the Lipizzaner horses seem to mimic this, too. It's all as posed and full of painterly cross-references as a frieze.

But then we walk on. Fairly soon we'll go and eat in the communal dining hall. The room's modern enough, light and airy and lined with pine. But it is not decorative. You wouldn't feel you were getting any more than you'd paid for. The exact same meal is served to everyone at once, and on the dot of seven. This seems to be a kind of post-communist compromise with market forces. On the one hand there are the dining-room staff, who've clearly worked here for decades and are set in their ways – which don't include much that you'd call customer service. On the other, commercial forces are being exerted by the coach-loads of Italian and Austrian pensioners who are our chief companions. On our first night here we asked the matron in charge of our section, the stout and unaptly named Jelena (it means *deer*), why we all had to eat the same thing. She laughed with incredulity – what would choice be for? *All* the food here is tasty – and whipped away our soup plates without breaking step.

For now, though, we walk and talk and the smell of S's TKP-brand Rodeo cigarette hangs in the still air like the first hint of autumn bonfires. All round us the oaks of Lipica grow tall in the clean air. The shallow karstic topsoil means they remain spindly. Between their trunks we can see, as well as white horses and boulders, *polje* dimples and *doline* declivities. Close cropping makes these especially visible here, and visitors unfamiliar with limestone country guess them to be the signs of lost human settlement, or bomb craters. Both of which, confusingly, also pock the slopes of the Karst.

But it's the self-fulfilling prophecy of erosion that has created these bowls and sinkholes in the bedrock. Some are no more than a couple of metres long. Others are much larger. One of the biggest on this estate is the Valley of Our Lady of Lourdes. It's a boat-shaped declivity, big enough to seat about 200 people, set between slopes thick with oak and beech. The trees create a canopy for wooden benches that have been lined up in the *doline* to await an audience.

This little theatre is also an outdoor shrine, set up in the second half of the nineteenth century by a grateful former manager of the stud. Karel Grünne believed that he owed his recovery from serious illness to daily visits to the place: the shrine he established is credited with a number of subsequent miracles, even though it was largely abandoned during the communist era. Garlanded with plastic flowers, a metre-high Virgin stands in a faux stone-effect niche at one end of the Valley. She's pallid, her plaster a little chipped; her statue isn't, in fact, quite equal to the place that bears her name. But the *doline* itself is full of sunlight and the soughing of leaves a hundred metres overhead. If you sit down and wait, after a while you get the curious sensation that you're in a stone boat; only the medium you're sailing through isn't water but air, and you're suspended not above but below it.

S flicks away his fag end and descends the Valley's stone steps reluctantly. He's wearing a sceptical expression as he joins me. His national church is Macedonian Orthodox, and he practises an indoor religion, inclined to icons, ritual observance and incense in the darkness. Tapers in racks for the living; tapers in racks at floor level for the dead. So this open-air, almost pantheistic strand of Catholic observance, which is carried out at shrines among birch woods in Poland, at country crossroads in Périgord, and here in the secret limestone places of the Karst, seems to him counterintuitive; not only unfamiliar, but possibly even blasphemous. It doesn't have any of the guarantors of true faith that he recognises: the presence of a priest, or the correct forms of words. The lichen creeping in yellow spirals across the rock wall by my head, the flycatchers twitching their tails and hopping from rock to rock in the retreating sunlight: these have not been organised by religion. We simply recruit them ourselves − if we can manage such hopeful attentiveness − to whatever the meaning is that we give such places.

Though he's not especially religious, S is superstitious enough to fear the consequences of meddling with wrong observance. He sits hunched in his jacket on the edge of a bench, shaking his head as he does when we disagree or he doesn't know what I'm saying. I don't argue back – aloud. But I am touched by such shrines. I like the feeling of prayer moving in these declivities and hidden valleys as if it were a mist. Perhaps I imagine it that way because this sort of religious practice seems a little foggy when it comes to doctrinal detail, more a feeling than a faith. I'm also aware that I don't completely understand it. Even the words with which people pray here are unfamiliar to me. But in Catholic Europe, as it's endured the centuries of its various wars, such outdoor prayer must always have been principally private, and sometimes secret too. The Valley gives me a feeling that I'll have again, years from now, in the Val du Calvaire in Périgord, a *polje* where P and I will walk between the hay bales one afternoon and feel uncannily as though we're interrupting something, though there is nothing and nobody there.

The former Yugoslavia's own recent wars of religion are a salutary reminder of how faith can go hand in hand with a nationalism that fetishes the 'folk' or *narod* and their countryside. But outdoor shrines like these are places for confidential, individual prayer; they have the force and intimacy of the confessional. They are where girls go when they're caught out by pregnancy or its lack; or where, later in life, they might return to mourn. The smell of fresh air seems to symbolise the intensity of such supplication.

Perhaps coming to places like this has always been primarily women's observance: perhaps that worries S too. I don't tell him that I came here daily while I was waiting for him to arrive; days when I was convinced by turn that he was gravely ill or miraculously recovered. Did I pray for his recovery, under a leaf canopy that shifted as if some giant breath were passing through it? 'Sem in se ne izprašujem zakaj', 'I Am And I Can't Ask Why', says Kosovel, of such moments:

> Beyond the cottages, fields and gardens
> as the dream shines on them,
> beyond narrow lanes, beyond fences
> silence stretches quietly across the fields
> I am and I can't ask why
> along with the cottages, fields and gardens

The Karst is the leafy, lingering odour of Boss cigarettes. It is voices on the still evening air as families and friends eat together outdoors. It's also the tannic, earthy taste of the local Teran wine. 'Teran' means *earth*, predictably enough; this Karst wine is pungent with everything that grows in its limestone soil. It's strong, never bland; a red that leaves no syrupy aftertaste but fires straight into the synapses. Teran is made from eponymous grapes that grow in the high vineyards between the little town of Sežana and the villages of Tomaj and Štanjel. These south-west facing slopes perch on the very brink of the northern Dinaric Karst plateau, overlooking the Italian littoral towards Trieste. Sea light streams straight up at them, bleaching the stone that lies crumbling but conspicuous on a red soil, the characteristic limestone *terra rossa*, at the feet of the vine rows.

Teran is best drunk at outdoor tables, with bread and grilled local *ćevapčići* ('little kebabs': actually skinless sausages) that taste freshly of charcoal and wild herbs. But in the late summer of 2004 we're passing through the Karst on a visit that hurries us away from such pleasures. S and I can only glimpse the famous vineyards as we're swept past them in an outsized, high-sided bus heading north in the direction of the Soča Valley. The road we're on is tightly flanked by stone walls that our bus squeezes between; dry-stone walls in a pale, greyish limestone that reminds me of England criss-cross the countryside between houses, gardens and fields. Unlike the flat, split stone that English dry-wallers use though, these walls are made of round stones, the way they are in the west of Ireland. Accordingly, each wall is only about four stones high – and is really just a long pile of boulders kept together by their own weight.

Over the coming years we're going to explore the hinterland of these villages and vineyards, a landscape where little family holdings have returned to woodland. Often the walls that mark such holdings have rolled apart completely, becoming nothing more than a stony margin, thick with moss, over which the forest animals pass freely to and fro: foxes and deer (*Jelena*! the road signs warn), boar and even the occasional brown bear or wolf.

This apparent neglect isn't pure laziness. After 1945, land holdings larger than forty-five hectares (of poor Karst region farming land: in some fertile areas, the holdings involved could be as small as twenty-five hectares) were nationalised in communist Yugoslavia. The collectivisation of individual peasant farmers' land was also attempted, but fiercely resisted right up until 1953, when the policy was abandoned and individual holdings were restored. The result of this mixed strategy was a patchwork landscape of large, socially owned farms and small peasant family holdings, often farmed part-time, which were deliberately kept unviable by a range of government policies. By the time those who were energetic enough to do so had reclaimed their family land, many possible heirs had drifted away to the towns in search of work.

Yet here and there we suddenly come across a field – often a *doline* – scooped out of the oak woods, the orange soil turned in ready furrows and, depending on the time of year, a crop of maize, or allotment rows of beans on canes, blackcurrant bushes and marigolds. The Slovenian for a field is a *polje* and it's no surprise that, in the Karst, geological *dolines* are often called *polje*. (The original Slovenian term *dolina* tends to be used here for more dramatic chasms.)

When we're out in the unclaimed woods surrounding these *polje*, I don't feel we're alone *in* so much as *with* them. As we walk, the trees pass one after another like points being made in a kind of cross-species dialogue. The air thrums with mosquitos and with jiggling clouds of midges. It's easy to see how this feeling could develop into a kind of pantheism. And some kind of pantheistic impulse does see Slovenians dress ritually in carnival masks, with costumes made of bearskins and sheepskins, red and blue streamers, *becoming* the natural world that surrounds them and the harvest that their livelihoods depend upon.

These country traditions, where they survive – as *kurenti* in the north-east of the country for example – are carried out with great good public humour; but also a sense of occasion. Like Carnival they occur mostly at the start of Lent even though, also like Carnival, they long predate that observance. Rather like English Morris dances, these traces of pre-Christian belief are honoured now as repositories of the national self, the historical Slovenian *narod*. They're meaningful, but no longer freighted with *religious* meaning.

S recognises in these old festivals a northern version of his own country's ethnology. Here in Slovenia, he points out as we ease into our seats for the display at yet another civic ceremony, there's altogether more white linen and lace on show than there would be in southern Serbia, Macedonia or Bulgaria. White bibs on the traditional costumes of the women and girls, lace handkerchiefs for effect, and (after the dancing) white linen to wrap the fresh bread in an upmarket 'traditional' restaurant. If on these occasions Slovenian women with their flashes of white resemble nothing so much as dippers (*Cinclus cinclus*) – he says – their Macedonian sisters, in darkly brocaded long waistcoats, must favour some altogether less chirpy bird. Heron perhaps?

I enjoy our wanders in the Karst woods. The right to roam, widely practised though not specifically enshrined in the Slovenian constitution, strikes me as novel and tremendous. But I'm a little afraid of the brown bears that live here. Though no one's actually seen them, everyone knows someone who has. Our friend Iztok, poet, philosopher and longhaired mountaineer, has one of the most convincing stories. Over a glass of Teran he settles in to tell us how a friend of his was cycling the high roads in the Julian Alps, up past the snowline where the tarmac gives way to gravel forestry tracks. As the friend swooped silently downhill, pumped on adrenaline, busy timing himself and avoiding potholes, he rounded a corner – and crashed straight into a bear. Which luckily was as bowled over, both literally and metaphorically, as he was. Iztok's friend got straight back on his bike, raced off – and survived with nothing worse than a couple of broken ribs to show for the experience.

One reason there are relatively few actual encounter stories is that to meet a bear tends to be pretty bad for the health. If a bear chooses to attack, even the most upbeat hikers' websites admit, there's little you can do. Though there *are* plenty of things you can do wrong. Try not, for example, to have your period, carry food, stumble on a nursing mother, be downhill from the bear, wear bright clothes, be too well-camouflaged, make a noise, be quiet, run away, fail to get away. Playing dead may help apparently; or alternatively so may leaping about, making masses of noise and appearing to be larger than you are. It seems to depend on the kind of day the bear is having.

Later, as he marches us through the Betanja woods to his favourite viewpoint, Iztok says the important thing to do is make plenty of noise, singing and talking as you walk, so that you never *surprise* a bear in the first place. She – or he, but somehow what I imagine is always a she-bear, full of maternal rage – attacks not because she thinks you'll be tasty but because you hadn't figured in her calculations and so your appearance is a threat. A bit like surprising a star in her dressing room.

My trouble with all of this is that it's so easy to imagine because in the – we can't say exactly primeval but still unpolluted, pre-industrial – woodlands of the Karst you are so palpably being watched. Behind every tree are creatures assessing your likely next move. It's easy to get spooked when a deer blunders away uphill though the undergrowth, *crish-crash*; even easier when it does not.

This is what happens late one July afternoon. Alone at last, S and I have found the perfect spot for a picnic. The main road through Matavun doglegs round one of the village *polje*. But behind the houses lie two much larger valleys. The level bottom of each stretches to five or six acres of thick calf-high meadow grass, flecked with buttercups, coltsfoot, and the small 'dock leaves' of sorrel, *Rumex acetosa*. Regular haymaking keeps them clean of tares and un-tussocky. Light, kept off elsewhere by leaf canopy, appears to pool in these contour-delineated meadows, giving them the appearance of an ideal. The spot we pick is in the furthest *polje,* under a trio of apple trees that suggest there was once an orchard here. S opens the wine and I unwrap a slab of deep-yellow, local cheese.

It's a beautiful afternoon, and we relax. Above us the cliff catches the sun and turns whitish-gold. Two honey buzzards, *Pernis apivorus,* spin out from it to circle lazily above us as if willing us to turn into carrion. We hear the shriek of a captured rabbit somewhere high on the clifftop; it carries in the calm air. Then it stops abruptly. Everything goes very still. Everything is so still, in fact, that it seems to be holding itself motionless. The usual undergrowth fussing of squirrels and deer has ceased. The birds seem to have frozen in the trees. The pneumatic rattle of a woodpecker – probably the green *Picus viridis* we glimpsed earlier in his lofting, lilting flight across the clearing – has stopped. So, further off, has the nagging laugh of a jay. No crows rise out of their treetop nests to mob the buzzards.

I know this kind of silence. It's the sort that arrives with a predator: a cat in the garden, a fox in the paddock. Almost immediately I'm on my feet. 'What's happening?' I ask S. 'Listen, everything's stopped.' S – oblivious, amorous – is reluctant to listen, and even more reluctant to relinquish our daybed among the tree roots. But we do; we make our way back along the tracks that skirt the valleys, alternately talking loudly to alert any bear that's in the neighbourhood, and falling silent to see whether we can hear anything, any hint or warning of a beast nearby.

When we get back to Irwin's *gostilna* ('hostelry': hear the old-fashioned English inside the Slovenian), nobody quite pooh-poohs our story. The village consensus is that such things *could* happen here, even if they usually don't. It's part perhaps of the rural perspective, a sense of the drama in the local. Irwin is only half joking when he offers us a coffee on the house.

We drink it gratefully, at a table under the vine, watching the village come back to itself for the evening. Cars pull up; people are returning home from work. The school bus disgorges three teenagers, two younger kids. One carries a football, which he immediately starts to bounce. Long after the echoes of the bus engine have died away, the *thud*, *thud* of his ball can be heard moving slowly uphill towards the hamlet of Betanje.

In summer 2004, as we sit on the bus through the vineyards, this afternoon when a predator – or maybe just the shadow of mortality – passes close to us in the woods of Matavun is still years in the future. In 2004 there are to be no picnics: we are at work. The bus is ferrying us to Štanjel for the annual reading in the castle courtyard.

In my memory of the day, we're all dazed with hangovers. Teran sticks to the neurons the way it smears a glass. The courtyard at Štanjel is handsome, but it's completely unshaded apart from the single giant magnolia tree that shelters the compère. Everything seems fractured and uncomfortable. The castle bar serves nothing but rakia and espressos: the boys from Ljubljana, and our silk-scarfed Austrian literary expert, have been drinking since before breakfast. A sound system is crackling its way through welcome speeches. The local audience sit unmoving and expressionless. There are many Balkan haiku on the programme. We slip away.

Štanjel's ruined castle crowns what looks at first glance like a ghost village. But that must be an illusion: hammering from a large house on the lane beside the curtain-wall has accompanied the readings. Many of the village's *stare hiše*, old houses, seem uninhabited; several appear to be immaculately prepped shells, where stacks of corrugated iron and sacks of sand suggest work that's in progress, albeit not today. These are holiday homes that wealthy Triestians – and Europeans from further west – have picked up cheap to turn into heritage chic. Others, already restored, sport blue shutters, willow-plaited hearts on their doors, and blue-and-white-check gingham pelmets at each window. The cars parked outside them are racy: low Italian speedsters, Ferraris and Alfa Romeos. S raises his eyes at these, though actually he doesn't have car envy. His own pink VW Beetle – hangover from a stint as a Balkan rock star – has been famous in Skopje for decades.

Štanjel blends into its karstic hillside. Its walls and roofs of pale limestone appear quarried from the very rock on which they stand. Unrestored, these houses gradually return to the landscape as boulders and stones littering the topsoil. How long would it take a place like this to disappear altogether? But the village has been astute, tapping into a tourist market that has exhausted the antiquities of Italy and southern France, and is searching for the next piquant, yet sunny, spot for its European holidays. Local planners are keen on heritage but comfortable with changes of use that turn barns and piggeries into luxury *gîtes*. The town councillors in Sežana, in whose hinterland Štanjel lies, are thinking ahead, and imagining a whole sophisticated tourist industry into being.

That they can do so has much to do with one man, Alexander P., a Karst-born visionary who combines the idealism and the pragmatism needed to present this region as an international attraction. He understands, because he genuinely loves the

Karst, that its future doesn't lie in the second division of cheap package tourism. Though it can provide the hotel and drinking complexes this kind of holidaymaker's looking for, with no sea, no clubbing and no shopping it will never be their first choice. Instead, Alexander's Karst will appeal to an altogether more bourgeois visitor. He's after the type of guest who eats traditional food on the vine-grown terrace of a *taverna* in Italy, here a *gostilna*; goes walking in Swiss – or Slovenian – Alpine meadows; and rents an historic villa in Tuscany one year, a *gîte* in the Midi the next, and a lovingly restored farmhouse in the Karst the third.

It's because of this vision, rather than any personal investment in such fields, that he channels public money to the arts, heritage and archaeology. This quiet internationalist speaks not a word of any foreign language except Russian. With his comb-over and slightly shabby blazer (worn in all weathers), he cuts a modest figure, always reluctant to give the opening speech at the innumerable conferences and festivals he initiates. He's less likely to be found in front of the microphone than behind the wheel of his old blue estate car, driving participants to and from airports and stations. This modesty is as infuriating as it is admirable. Try talking to Alexander about himself – his own motivation and background, or his life story – and he'll refer you to someone, anyone, else; including the translator through whom you're trying to converse.

Just once, I think I've caught him. It's lunchtime and he's sitting alone at a table outside Marko's hamlet *gostilna*, nursing a coffee. The sunlit terrace around him is bare; he has his back to the dramatic view over a karstic gorge. The only other person on the terrace is Marko's six-year-old, who's teasing the hotel cat, and Alexander seems glad when we join him. After a few minutes I bring up the topic of his work, and S translates my questions. But all too soon Alexander is once again referring us to someone who's published a collection of traditional Karst songs, someone else who was part of the team that discovered Neolithic arrow heads in the Soča valley, and a third person who may hold the key for the church at Gradišče pri Divači, where there are astonishing fifteenth-century frescoes.

Seduced in spite of ourselves, some time later we walk the rim of dramatic Velika Dolina, the Great Collapse or Great Chasm, to the hamlet of Gradišče pri Divači; where we find the key to St Helena's Church is indeed held by an elderly farmer. He's expansively proud of his local heritage, and he tells us so at length while strolling up to the church with us to unlock it.

On this sunny day, the simple, almost domestic nave of St Helena's is a shock of cool. And the frescoes *are* astonishing. It's not that they're vast, or sophisticated – they are neither – but, because they aren't quite like anything else either of us has seen before, they defy us to react or even to name what we are seeing. In the aisle-less nave of the essentially Romanesque church they make a simple enough frieze. But their idiom seems halfway between naïve, vernacular art and the kind of 'high' art usual in churches. Christ steps out of the tomb in Gethsemane with saucer eyes and a face devoid of expression. Yet each panel is a sophisticated portrayal of action-in-action. Even the inert, crucified Christ hangs between a busily praying angel and a Mary who wrings her hands with real physiological verisimilitude.

The scenes are alive with colour, their greens and blues particularly fresh: perhaps this is because the frescoes were only rediscovered in the 1950s. The Three Kings, journeying on horseback to see the Christ Child, travel with an entourage including buglers, fools, cooks and huntsmen. At least one leaves behind a lady wife, who waves him off from a turreted castle. They're accompanied on their pilgrimage along the north wall by playful, bounding creatures both tame and wild: hare, dogs, pelicans and wild boar. Elsewhere, Christ enters a Gothic-windowed Jerusalem by way of a splendid, red and gold carpet. Everything is portrayed as slightly rounded, even plumped up, as if to say that the *fullness* of life should be celebrated.

The painting was made around 1490 by 'Magister Johannes de Kastua', the High Gothic *maestro* known in Slovenian as *Janez iz Kastva*. He's famous for the frescoes that cover the interior walls and ceilings of the fortified church at Hrastovlje, south of here, which include a Dance of Death and trompe l'oeil capitals on the nave pillars. They were rediscovered in 1949, became a landmark on the international tourist trail in Yugoslavian times, and are now a UNESCO World Heritage site. Little Gradišče pri Divači, population fewer than two dozen, may have hoped for a similar renaissance. That hasn't happened. But with its strangely cosy emptiness this humble church, into which the leaves drift with the autumn breeze, makes faith seem for a moment close at hand and somehow neighbourly.

The almost naïve frescoes at Gradišče pri Divači illustrate how recently Slovenia has emerged as a nation state. Until the end of the First World War, when it was declared part of the Kingdom of the Serbs, Croats and Slovenes, 'Slovenia' did not figure fully in either official government business or high art culture: it was still a vernacular regional rather than a national identity. Slovene art was folk art. To be a Slovenian artist painting a church fresco in the late fifteenth century would therefore mean both being the recipient of a local honour and imagining oneself into the great tradition of artists from over the Italian border. Not that 'Janez iz Kastva' was exactly 'Slovenian' in the modern sense, though he was a fellow citizen of the Hapsburg Empire (from 1466, anyway): his hometown of Kastav, close to Rijeka, lies on the Istrian coast of Croatia.

So in 1490, when Janez painted the frescoes at Gradišče pri Divači, Slovenian identity was contained not so much within national borders as within the language itself. It was further reinforced by the feudal demarcation of territories by aristocratic families such as the Celje. Yet Slovenian, like other Slav languages (including Macedonian, S reminds me), went largely unregarded by the region's ruling class. They spoke the imperial language of German and, as educated Europeans, wrote and ruled in Latin, which was also the language of the Catholic Church.

Slovenian, dismissed as not only peasant speech but a mere Southern Slavonic *dialect* at that, remained largely unregarded even while it was the everyday language of the population. Or rather, the everyday language*s*, since standardisation would not arrive until the second half of the sixteenth century, with Lutheranism's characteristic production of vernacular texts. It was the Protestant preacher Primož Trubar (1508–86) who – though he spent much of his adult life in Germany – wrote the first books published in Slovenian, and who is credited with much of this work of linguistic consolidation.

As in other emerging nation states – Poland and Romania are striking examples of this, boasting respectively of Adam

Mickiewicz (1798–1855) and Mihai Eminescu (1850–99) – what next changed the language's fortunes was poetry. Slovenia's national poet France Prešeren has his own statue in his own square in the centre of Ljubljana. Continuing the work of turning Slovenian into a language in which, as the scholar Joza Mahnič has put it, everything can be said, he chose it for his highly wrought, Romantic verse. In so doing he explored and developed its resources to such an extent that he turned it into not just a language of literacy, but something truly literary. Though he experimented with traditional Slovenian folksong and ballad forms, he was in touch with Europe-wide, high art convention, and it was he who brought forms such as the sonnet into Slovenian.

Born in 1800, dead at forty-nine: Prešeren's was a Romantic's life and death. He succumbed to liver disease after years of heavy drinking. Despite this, the mainstream of literary history nearly passed him by. By the time he was experimenting with his first, unpublished verses in the 1820s, Lord Byron had already pressed on south from Italy and Switzerland into the Balkans, bypassing Slovenia in search of Albania and Greece, and the latter's armed struggle against the Ottoman Empire.

But Prešeren was luckier in every way than was his literary heir, Srečko Kosovel, the precocious modernist genius who died in 1926 at the age of twenty-two from meningitis. Kosovel was born in Sežana and spent his childhood nearby in the Karst village of Tomaj before being sent away to study in Ljubljana at the age of twelve. The year was 1916. He went to board in the capital not only for the sake of his education but to remove him from the danger of the nearby Soča Front, scene of some of the most brutal fighting of the First World War, which still casts a shadow over the region.

In 1929, the Kingdom of Serbs, Croats and Slovenes would become the Kingdom of Yugoslavia, and after the Second World War Slovenia, recovering from its annexation by Germany, Italy and Hungary (not to mention of a tiny rump by Croatia), would be a founder member of Yugoslavia: first the Federal Republic, then the non-aligned Socialist Federal Republic. But in 1920, when Kosovel was sixteen, the Treaty of Rapallo annexed most of the Karst heartland to Italy, and – together with nearby Trieste, where many Slovenes had settled – it was subject to forced Italianisation. The use of Slovenian was forbidden: and Kosovel's father was a teacher of Slovenian. Censorship and repression: it's an unexpectedly shocking version of the city where James Joyce and Italo Svevo were then living and writing, a Trieste whose cosmopolitanism we assume.

Large numbers of middle-class Slovenes emigrated, either to Serbia or to South America. Those who stayed suffered. Local history in the Karst is about more than funny moustaches and the arrival of the penny-farthing. Annexation meant that, once the Second World War was underway, the civilian Slovene population had nothing to protect it from mass deportation to internment camps in Italy and on the Italian-occupied island of Rab. But countrymen make good resistance fighters. The communist partisan movement this brutality helped inspire would eventually grow to liberate the entire country and provide the basis of its post-war organisation.

Srečko Kosovel managed to live through the disturbances of the early 1920s and still develop into a great poet of the limestone landscape, as well as an avant-garde experimenter. His version of the geology of home is about as far from W. H. Auden's 'In Praise of Limestone' as it's possible to imagine. While the British poet visualises a friable, highly accommodating and even entertaining landscape, the Slovene portrays the Karst – and through it, the world – as intractable, dense and mysterious. Limestone country provides him with both the symbols and style to create a condensed, lapidary way of writing that's by turns impressionist and Imagist and often – against all the rules – both at once.

No other poet would find a way back to this use of rock as source until half a century later when Mak Dizdar, exploring the Bosnian limestone landscape, turned repeatedly to rocks and tombstones as sources of hieratic meaning, most famously in *Stone Sleeper* (1966). His French contemporary, Eugène Guillevic, used the menhirs and limestone landscapes of Brittany in similar ways, for example in 1961's *Carnac*.

Every poet longs to be brought back to life by their own verse. For Kosovel, in 'Resurrection – Death':

> In the centre of the green rose of fire
> I search for beauty, but everything is alien,
> the air motionless, the wind glass –
> and yet – spring …

How to make what's very old into something new? This is the work of a writer who understands that the liveliness of tradition doesn't come from where and how it originated, but from its use today. That's true of Karst traditions too. If, like Kosovel, you emerge from a community that still lives a tough, traditional farming life, you witness that life as contemporary reality and not as inert pastoral cliché, the genteel fantasy of some middle-class water-colourist.

Even today the Karst remains a tough place to live. At any time of year its high villages can be battered by the Bora or *burja*, the cold north wind which blows off the Alps. Western Slovenia enjoys a Mediterranean climate, with long warm summers and mild winters. But it's moderated by Slovenia's inland climate, which is continental: in other words its summers are warm and winters cold. Temperatures in January average several degrees below freezing; in July they usually reach the high twenties. But even in the height of such summers the Bora blows with tremendous, insistent force for two or three days at a time. It's a *katabatic,* or downhill, condition that occurs when cold air from the mountainous heart of the continent meets the warm air of coastal convection. The heavier cold air is pulled downhill by nothing more complex than gravity.

Such humourless, dry-cold winds terrorise the whole northern shore of the Mediterranean. In France, the wind that blows from the north-east is called the mistral after the Occitan for 'master'; and in all the languages of the northern Mediterranean shore this is the 'master' wind. When the Bora arrives it seems utterly wilful. It makes dogs and children restless, it goads the livestock in their barns, and its ceaseless, oceanic seething makes humans of all ages feel obscurely threatened and at the same time eager to do *something* – without knowing exactly what.

When the 'master' wind blows everyone else closes their shutters, but S and I open our bedroom window wide and sit on the sill to watch the trees churn all along the *doline* below us, showing the pale undersides of their leaves in a sort of arboreal Mexican wave. There's a tremendous soughing, as if the wind is carrying some huge, collective memory towards or away from us.

Perhaps that's why it makes us restless. It's a sound that says life goes on elsewhere, or in the past, or is yet to come. It challenges us to take stock. It makes us want to change the life we lead. And who's to say how longing works? Maybe the second-homers who fall in love with the depopulated villages of the Karst understand them just as deeply as Kosovel did when he returned, again and again, to this region in the verse he wrote while exiled in Ljubljana.

Štanjel is all of eleven kilometres from Kosovel's native village of Tomaj. As S and I walk out of the castle courtyard into that long ago, lost summer morning, swallows dart shrieking from eave to eave almost between our heads. The main village street winds along the brow of the hill, past the wide-fronted stone houses. Where it's been freshly cut – here for a lintel, there in a patch of new wall – the stone is dazzlingly white. Elsewhere, it's weathered to a light dove grey. There's a warm smell of dust and rosemary as we stroll uphill, enjoying the school's out sense of obligation skipped.

S is keen to scrounge a light. Two guys in dusty singlets are building a terrace outside one of the houses. They pause from shovelling sand to lend him their lighter, and describe with relish the plans the owner of the place, a Triestian, has for this hillside garden: terrace, steps, a swimming pool. He's left his project in good hands; Slovenians pride themselves on their workmanship.

Assured that we understand this, the builders now stop for a proper fag break and introduce themselves as brothers called Aleš and Gregor. Wiry, darkly tanned Aleš is the elder. 'But not much older,' Gregor insists, speaking up as the brains of the operation. It was Gregor who got them this job: or rather, the job three houses ago that led to this one. The brothers themselves can't afford to move to a village like Štanjel, although only a couple of years ago it would have been possible. But back then – Aleš intervenes, shaking his head – nobody thought such things could be done. These houses were unsaleable. They'd fallen into ruin because no one wanted to live up here on the windswept Karst, where there is no work. Banks wouldn't advance credit to private individuals to speculate on developing the place, and the high standards of Slovenian craftsmanship stopped larger building contractors from simply sweeping through these high valleys, making a quick buck and moving on.

As Aleš presents his thesis, scratching his head behind one ear in what's clearly a characteristic gesture of rumination, it's confirmed by the state of the houses all around us. Those that have been repaired are exquisitely finished. All are large by British standards: old and new alike, Slovenian houses always surprise me with their size. Everywhere, from village to suburb, the characteristic new-build is a colour rendered breezeblock construction sporting a shallow-pitched, red-tiled roof and, usually, a first-floor front balcony.

The results aren't beautiful, but they are spacious, smart, and for the most part noticeably smartly kept, too. After neighbouring Croatia, Slovenia has the highest proportion of people living in detached houses in the whole of the EU (in 2014 it was 65 per cent). As in all the post-communist countries, the percentage of owner-occupation with no mortgage is high: at over 60 per cent it's more than double the UK rate. Here, like other small, much-conquered nations – I find myself thinking of Wales – the domestic assumes exceptional importance. It's as if a turn inward to the family, that last and most local of communities, could protect individuals and the lives they treasure from the madness of world affairs.

We thank the brothers, and leave them to it. Perhaps – S speculates – since Slovenes are a nation with a strong farming legacy, they also tend to develop a farmer's traditional canniness with property? There's a certain consistency, after all, between the way Aleš and Gregor build, and the way Alexander and his colleagues are developing the Karst. Even on this morning in 2004, heritage and ecotourism have already revived the region's fortunes markedly in the thirteen years since Slovenian independence. The new Slovenia is quickly developing an ecotourism infrastructure out of its expansive – and sports-friendly – landscape, a network of certified farm accommodation, and what we'd now call Slow Food. (*Slow Food?* asks S, incredulously.) All of the country is proudly GM-free; much of what's sold and eaten throughout Slovenia is also organic.

Thirty kilometres away from Štanjel in Matavun, for example, Irwin runs Pr Vncki. In part a typical young-ish entrepreneur, he's also a gifted chef with a real feel for the land: how to cultivate it, its traditions, and the pleasures of a life spent on it. This combination of business flair with a love of all things rural is typically Slovenian. Irwin's background is in hospitality, but of a surprising kind. When market freedoms arrived after Independence, he opened the first nightclub in Sežana. The most desirable young bachelor on the Karst, he picked a shy schoolgirl, later an academic geographer, to court and marry. A few years later, Sežana's Municipal Council bought Pr Vncki, which had become a seedy, failing hostel despite being pretty much the only local facility for visitors to Škocjan's UNESCO World Heritage Site caves. Irwin bid successfully for the franchise, and he and Tamara moved in, turned the business around, and started a family. Now he opens five nights a week in season, each evening cooking only a single set meal made entirely from local ingredients. Dumplings, venison, *jota* (stew) with fresh herbs, and air-dried Karst ham are staples. And, of course, he makes excellent Slovenian coffee: thick, sludgy and chestnut brown.

Irwin is great company: it's one secret of his professional success. Tanned by the long Slovenian summer, in his shorts and flip-flops and with his plaited leather bracelet, he could be a beach bum or a surfing instructor. He's spent time in the off-season selling restaurant gear in Australia, and makes no secret of how much he loved that country. This surprises S. When Irwin tells us how he liked the laid-back, no-worries-mate attitude to business in Oz S, to whom Slovenia still seems like a Westernised paradise, is really struck. 'But truly, what is the difference?' he asks, leaning forward to accept a light. Irwin laughs. *Nema problema* is all very well, but it's a promise, not a process. Australia is less bureaucratic than the former Yugoslavia. Also, it's not corrupt.

S and I have noticed a fear of Big Government on our visits to the Karst. It's easy to see how farming the stony littoral breeds a spirit of resilient self-sufficiency. Easy too to guess how that has sunk down into the culture and re-emerged as a passion for decentralisation. Slovenia is a small country – you could work in Ljubljana but still commute home to the Karst in under two hours – so everyone who choses to remain out here all year round feels some positive resistance to city life, as well as a special empathy for farming and the land.

Irwin, for example, teaches his three-year-old how to blow on seeds before you plant them so that they will germinate for you. Now the little boy has grown the tallest sunflower in the village on his father's vegetable allotment. This strip of soil, with its topplingly abundant parsley and tomatoes, is set into Jarko's top field. It provides all the herbs and most of the salad leaves for Irwin's *gostilna* kitchen.

Every year Jarko clears the patch for Irwin: a quick up and down with the farrow, one two. It's a gesture of pure neighbourliness, for Irwin pays him no rent. But the old farmer has made his calculations. If Irwin thrives he brings custom to the village, including to Jarko's own *sobe*, or *pension* rooms, which Irwin recommends as his first 'overflow'. Pr Vncki has only two bedrooms: not enough to sustain its own evening opening even in high season, so Irwin in turn needs Jarko's *sobe* to keep his business thriving. The older man's own children and grandchildren followed the trajectory marked out for them by excellent Yugoslav education, and now live in the capital. But Irwin, Tamara and their two boys mean young blood coming into the village and keeping it alive.

Slovenian identity is so historically rooted in agriculture that even politicians and government wonks can't help but have a certain feel for how the countryside works. In a way this is a feeling for childhood itself, since even Slovenians growing up in towns often return to some form of extended family home in the village for the long summer school holidays. That must be one of the rare benign legacies of communism, which believed it could abolish the inequality of women by offering educational parity and employment (though not, of course, equal pay). Mothers out at work all day meant summer holidays during which children got sent away to stay with grandparents in the country, where daily working life took place closer to the home and could be combined with keeping an eye on the kids: city children could roam freely, safe from urban dangers if not from the hazards of the farmyard or of the natural world.

There's an entire literary subgenre, in Slovenia and the other countries of former Yugoslavia, that recalls being sent back to the village for the holidays. The Serbian-born Slovenian avant-gardist Andrej Brvar, for example, became a philologist as a result of his bilingual upbringing, and his long poem 'A Little Odyssey' evokes a daylong journey 'home' across a country unified by its countryside:

> And we travel on. And everywhere,
> everywhere I look, there's corn and corn and corn with
>   the little roots holding it up
> you can see them, and we're on a bridge …
>   And again everywhere,
> everywhere I look corn corn corn which the wind
>   brings to life
> its long spear-like leaves wave to me, shining and silver.

Slovenian countryside isn't the middle-class preserve it's becoming in Britain (although go tell that to those living in rural poverty), nor the collective unconscious it can represent for the urban French. It's understood to be basic and essential. Contemporary Slovenian literature, art and film is full of snapshots of maize or plums that sit oddly, for a British reader, among its postmodern gestures, and seem more radically out of place in the sophistication of contemporary Ljubljana than they would in, say, the Macedonian capital.

S shrugs and agrees. The city sits *in* the countryside. Nova Gorica, the town that builder-brothers Aleš and Gregor call home, lies like Ljubljana in a river basin. Unlike the chocolate-box Slovenian capital, it's a claustrophobic and depressing town, built on ghosts. Here in the wooded valley of the Soča, the limestone plateau gives way suddenly to the scene of some of the worst fighting of the First World

War, where some 1.7 million people lost their lives. It's an unimaginable figure; and all the more grotesque because the entire river is less than 150 kilometres long.

Gorizia itself, perched on a limestone bluff above the Soča-Isonzo river, remains in Italian hands to this day. This is the border region that the Italian modernist poet Giuseppe Ungaretti wrote about while fighting here. It's also the setting for Ernest Hemingway's 1929 novel of masculinity and loss, *A Farewell to Arms*. Both writers explore a particular claustrophobia along with the terror and exhaustion of war. Hemingway's lovers are trapped in a dance of death however hard they try to escape. Ungaretti's short-lined, tight poems seem trapped in a landscape, and a nightmare, from which there's no exit. Even the actual dark, dampish villages – Plave, Gorenje Polje, Ajba – that huddle below the treeline in the Soča valley bottom are claustrophobic with the memory of war. If I were Aleš and Gregor, I'd want nothing more than to escape to the bright, bare Karst uplands.

Kras, their Slovenian name, comes from the Romans' second-century Latinisation, *Carsus*, of the old Slav root word for stone or rock, *ka-*. The name appears, as *Garst*, in records from as early as the twelfth century; but it's since the nineteenth century that Slovenia's Karst region has given its name to this form of limestone country wherever it occurs in the world, from Australia to the Philippines, and from Spain to Egypt. In this sense, all such landscapes everywhere are a Slovenian phenomenon.

Yet even as its name continues to spread, the landscape itself is being depopulated, following the pattern for European highlands. If it were not on the way from Ljubljana to Trieste, the Karst would certainly not be served as it is by the international

Highway E61, which cuts through its textbook contours and gives long-distance commuters a unique geology lesson. On either side are the oirignal landmarks whose Slovenian names are given by karstologists to similar formations wherever they appear. Here are the sudden *dolines*, the ravines that delineate collapses caused by underground streams and caves: the Slovenian for collapse or subsidence is *dolina*. Here are the caves themselves, the *jama*: everywhere the geological term for the potholes known colloquially as *abîme* in French. Here are the crater-like basins of *polje*, studding the landscape with the fields for which they're named.

From our room in Jarko's farm, we can see his *polje* beyond the lane, on the other side of a low wall. It's a wide dimple full of good grass kept for hay. This is fine, fertile soil. Along the barn walls, in plots of chestnut-coloured earth cut from the edges of hay meadows, or in chicken-wired back yards, sunflowers, maize and marrows grow alongside peppers, tomatoes and dahlias tied up with string. Flowers threaten to overgrow the houses in Kosovel's Tomaj, too. There, the limestone houses are stuccoed, and the stucco punctuated by painted shutters and relieved by the impedimentia of ground-floor terraces. As everywhere in Southern and Eastern Europe, the Slovenian *terasa* is no raised paving but is an open-sided outdoor 'room'. Old or new, every house has its terrace with a vine and plastic chairs, benches, a table with an oilcloth and perhaps a bottle on it, and the bric-a-brac of gardening.

One afternoon in verdant Tomaj, S and I step through a door whose green paint is peeling badly and that's set in a wall built not of the usual dry-stone boulders but of dressed and mortared limestone blocks. It feels like the start of an old, familiar story. We find ourselves in a walled orchard. Morning glory climbs the walls of the house that faces us beyond the trees. On either side of us are fig trees dropping their fruit onto the grass for wasps to work it over.

We're greeted by shouts from the terrace. We squint, and make out Barbra and Josip, scarcely visible beyond the brightness, sitting in the shade of a thick-trunked vine that clearly hasn't been pruned in years. This is Paradiso, their much-loved 'real' home. They can't live here fulltime, they tell us as they pour tumblers of homemade slivovitz. But Josip comes down and stays for weeks at a go when he's writing. 'It's wonderful to escape,' says Barbra, mildly. She has to be in Ljubljana Monday to Friday for her job at the Writers' Union. Today she exudes her usual miraculous aura of calm; though she's thin, and is smoking too much as usual. It's a shock to learn that she isn't happy at work. Still, she and Josip – a late marriage, and they clearly adore each other – have created an intimate, living paradise here.

Josip, a philosopher as well as a poet and short-story writer, is thoughtful; nervy. Lean and bearded, he too smokes continually, and with such peculiar intensity that he seems to be arguing with the rollup between his lips. He's suffered, in the new Slovenia, from the fact that he isn't ethnically Slovene but Bosnian. When this country became independent, many of the people living here were not ethnic Slovenes, though they were full citizens of Yugoslavia. Suddenly, that contracted state stopped at a new national border; and their citizenship stopped with it. Several of our friends lost their jobs. Zdravko, librarian at the handsome Slovenian National Library in Ljubljana, went back to Banja Luka, where he and his sons became caught up in the Bosnian wars. Boris, a Bulgarian filmmaker and haiku writer married to a Slovenian, has not worked since he was rounded up and interned. Now released, he's campaigned for all those who still languish beyond the margins of official narratives about a free, modern Slovenia.

While the guys talk politics, Barbra takes me up the sloping hillside garden to the newest tree in the orchard, a young quince which is fruiting this year for the first time. The large pale fruit, their skin lightly dotted with speckles like a Golden Delicious apple, are pear-shaped but much larger and fleshier than any I've ever seen. 'Smell it, smell the skin,' she encourages me. 'It's the *most* evocative smell. When I was a child, there was a quince tree outside my bedroom window. I remember this smell so much. It means summer.' A year from now Barbra will be dead, her friends convinced that workplace bullying gave her the cancer that killed her. Josip will be adrift, drinking and disappearing for days at a time. And S, the one we thought would be first to go, will still be alive.

He's here beside me now, zipping up his hoodie, ready for the trip to the caves that we feel we must make in order to do justice to the Karst. For here, just as in Tourtoirac, limestone means caves. There are more than 7,000 in this country, and more than 450 kilometres of them have been explored. We've already been to the castle built in the mouth of the cave at Predjama ('Pre-cave') and been told about the 'Man Fish', *človeška ribica*, that exists only in the limestone caves below this handsome Renaissance building, and nowhere else in the world. (This turns out to be not quite true: it lives in other limestone freshwater caves in this immediate region too.)

At one level the olm, *Proteus anguinus*, to give it its proper names, is a feeble thing about thirty centimetres in length, blind, and a pale pink that verges on transparent. It scuttles and darts in its dark habitat, using something like magnetism as well as its unusually sharp hearing and sense of smell to steer between the rocks. Despite being long called a fish, it's really an exclusively water-dwelling amphibian, with 'toes' on its forelimbs and hind feet – as well as gills – that seems caught forever at the evolutionary moment when creatures crawled out of the primeval waters: it's still nearly a fish, but as it were a fish with hands. The olm looks like a creature out of the metamorphic imagination of some mediaeval artist; from the margin of one of Janez iz Kastva's frescoes, perhaps. Yet it's perfectly adapted to life in the subterranean streams of the cave system, where the temperature stays a steady eight to ten degrees all year round. *Proteus anguinus* can live for a century and go without food for ten years at a time. Why ever would it evolve further?

The cave complex at Postojna is at least twenty-five kilometres long, and the River Pivka that helped form it flows on to join the River Rak at Planina Cave, in what's among the largest underground confluences in Europe. The whole thing then turns into the River Unica – which emerges to become (eventually, as it flows through the capital) the River Ljubljanica. That's plenty of territory for a thirty-centimetre monster that nothing – and nobody – wants to eat.

S is mildly claustrophobic, and the olm famously shy, so we forewent the splendours of Predjama. But now we're going to try our reluctant best to be tourists. The UNESCO-designated Škocjan Caves, *Škocjanske Jame*, are probably the Karst's most famous. The last time S visited them he was a teenager at youth camp. Personally, I find all caves a little disappointing. I'm in awe of the – to me – incomprehensible courage and curiosity of potholers. But I never feel that the dream of what Samuel Taylor Coleridge in 'Kubla Khan' calls 'caves of crystal and of ice' is met by the rather dull yellowish reality of stalactites and stalagmites. As for the names discoverers and custodians give the more freakish and crooked formations: surely these attempts to make them more interesting are an *admission* of dullness?

Nevertheless, here we are at the cave entrance. The guides interrogate our group: do we have heart conditions? Claustrophobia? Asthma? Are we fit enough to complete a three-kilometre walk? They remind us that if we're taken ill underground the alarm can't be raised until someone reaches the surface. They tell us to stay together. They're stern about not taking photos (but they can see, of course, that everyone is clutching a mobile phone). Flash lighting helps destroy the cave environment, which relies on darkness to preserve the dampness that is the 'life' of its limescale formations. Dried out by the light, this unique site would cease to grow and would die. 'You can buy very nice pictures, much better professional pictures, in the shop afterwards.' Light is a pollutant, like our breath and above all our skin. We must not touch. 'Please, respect the cave.'

We step into the dark: jaunty at first but falling quiet as we leave behind a cement entrance built in the 1930s, and step onto the first of a whole series of contemporary steel walkways that are suspended, sometimes a few centimetres, sometimes hundreds of metres, above the sloping rock floors. The strong torches of the guides play on walls ahead of us, and movement-sensitive lighting follows our progress through the caves.

Here are squat, reddish stalactites that look like termite mounds. Now we look down and through rock trays supporting dozens of pale squiggles which resemble those little blown-glass ornaments that were popular souvenirs in the Seventies.

We come across the River Reka, and stand above cauldrons of cold spume while the guides explain how these caves flood when there's high water. The water level doesn't simply rise, covering first one rung and then another of the escape ladder they indicate above us. Instead, it comes as a surge that completely fills chamber after chamber. This is why the cave complex is closed to the public when there has been rain. I try not to think what this is doing for S's claustrophobia.

We pass through the Silent Cave, Paradise, and the Great Hall. At last we enter the set piece with which this theatrical complex ends. The Murmuring Cave is immense, its roof a hundred metres above us. The spidery steel frame of the walkway with its steps and suspended bridge clings to one wall. Below us is a scene out of Gustave Doré. Water cascades violently over rock steps and through the narrow chasms it has created. The river needs this force: it will travel on another thirty-four kilometres underground, only emerging to join the sea at Duino.

> In Xanadu did Kubla Khan
> A stately pleasure-dome decree:
> Where Alph, the sacred river, ran
> Through caverns measureless to man
> Down to a sunless sea.

…though Samuel Taylor Coleridge's orientalist fantasy is not quite apt for the balmy Adriatic.

The cave forms a huge auditorium – and the thundering water is symphonic. Additionally, now that we're approaching the final chamber, Schmidl Hall, we've come into the area that's populated by bats. They clot the smooth lines of the cave roof like starlings on some imposing urban monument.

I love the name for these bat dormitories: *hibernacula*.

What we can see here is probably the *Miniopterus schreibersii*, or bent-wing, colony that migrates between here and Predjama, although this cave also has roughly equal numbers of the long-fingered bat, *Myotis capaccinii*. Occasionally one of these sleepily teeming creatures drops down to check whether we've managed to bring any insects with us in the halo of our body heat. Its turning flight is brisk but casual, almost a flopping motion. An American girl at the front of the group squeals in protest, 'It's a bat!' Gallantly, the guides flash their torches like light sabres up into the roof space above our heads.

Locals hold – or so Iztok, who believes that pretty much everything originates in Slovenia, tells us – that Dante Alghieri may have visited Škocjan's caves during his years of exile from Florence, and have been inspired by them to produce his vision of the *Divine Comedy*. I'm not sure that this great cave can really be said to resemble his *Inferno*. It *is* roughly bowl-shaped – spherical, if you count the roof space – but it's certainly not spiral. True, our walk through the cave system has felt at times like walking a labyrinth. That's especially the case now, as we pass through the final constriction into a large dry hall and see ahead of us, filling the cave mouth, the coloured world outside. But Dante and his peers couldn't possibly have taken the route we have, enabled as it is by twenty-first-century engineering.

Not that the caves at Škocjan were unknown in past centuries: on the contrary. The huge mouth of Schmidl Hall is an unignorable invitation that's been taken up by locals for centuries. The large caves of the Karst have been used in a variety of ways. Nearby Vilenica was the first tourist cave in the world, its earliest visitors recorded in 1633 when Count

Petazzi gave it to the nearby village of Lokev to manage. Postojna overtook Vilenica in the tourist stakes in the nineteenth century, when Archduke Ferdinand's 1819 visit heralded an era of intensive exploitation, which would include the early use of underground trains (from 1872) and electric light (in 1884). Nevertheless, Vilenica has come from behind, hosting an annual poetry festival ceremony every September since 1986, and in recent years a Christmas mass.

A level-floored hall with trestle seating, a stage and electricity, the main cave at Vilenica is reached by several flights down an iron staircase. It's cold, of course, and it is slow torture to wait on the austere wooden seating during interminable Slav ceremonial speeches. Festival organisers distribute slivovitz in little plastic cups, the kind dentists keep for mouthwash after they've done their worst. The drink is supposed to keep us warm. S, too polite to grumble in the Western way, is looking yellow, as he does when he's unwell, and he raises an eyebrow wryly as he lifts his dental beaker in a toast. Can conditions in the cave always have been so uncomfortable? Until the Second World War it was used for village dances: surely cheerless, hatted and scarfed affairs. Once the war had started, treasures from the national collections were stored here and in caves across the Karst.

What the guides at Škocjanska Jame don't tell us in their opening spiel is that the promised funicular lift at the end of the walk will be out of order, and that we'll have to walk back along the length of Velika Dolina, the Great Chasm, to the old emergency staircase. The funicular rises through eighty metres, but the *doline* is nearly one hundred and fifty metres high. By the time we get to the top, sweat stands out whitely on S's forehead. *Velika* indeed. This mighty hole in the ground entails 413 hectares of heritage park (population: sixteen). The gorge is shaped like a boomerang, with the huge natural entrance of the cave centred on its upper margin. The surrounding park also contains a Mala Dolina – Little Doline – and the Okroglica *abime*, a sinkhole in the heart of Škocjan village.

Opposite the entrance to Schmidl Hall is a scramble of viewpoint, where foxgloves and primulas grow in cracks of white stone newly exposed by surface erosion. When we come here with Iztok, he stands so near the edge and talks at such length that I think I'm going to faint. Below him the cliff falls away steeply – but not quite sheer. A hundred metres or so below us is a ledge spilling over with couch grass, hart's-tongue ferns, dwarfish, self-seeded birch and hornbeam saplings. The same distance below that again, a path cut into the rock worms its way around the *doline*. Below again, and we can see the outdoor version of the spumy, pale turquoise River Reka. (*Reka* means 'river', so this is the River River, named as if we were in Eden and it were the first and only stream.)

The park footpaths are cut from turf. Near the information centre they've been gravelled, but most have a natural pavement, created by rock and stones lying almost directly beneath the grass. A jumble of blue *Campanula justiniana* and yellow *Ranunculus pospichalii* are everywhere among the boulders and couch grass: Slovenia's colourful wildflowers are part of an ecosystem still relatively un-depleted by atmospheric pollution. But by the time we admire this view with Iztok, I know many more things about S than I did that summer morning, years ago, when we walked up through Štanjel together. I know, for example, that he's colour blind, and that this is why the flowers don't interest him.

I also know how ill he is. The main trail in Škocjanske Jame Park rises gently enough to nurse even a visitor as unfit as S through the first few hundred metres. We pass under Scots pines – their needles carpet the path and silence the annoying click of my trainers – before achieving the wide skirting wall of the Princess Stephanie Viewpoint. It was built in the 1880s for one of those imperial visits to their Slav dominions that in 1914 would prove fatal to the Austrian Empire, in the person of Stephanie's brother-in-law the Archduke Ferdinand, as well as to millions of ordinary Europeans. The glossy information brochure that we pick up at the park's combined ticket-office-cum-banqueting hall tells us that the princess was delighted by the view. Mention of the imperial restroom which was also built especially for her visit makes S laugh harder than I've heard him do for months.

The view *is* impressive, all the more striking because our awe descends rather than ascends: we're looking down on a gorge rather than up at mountains. On the opposite side of the Velika Dolina is Škocjan church, its tower topped by a spire that looks and acts like a fingerpost. Pointing up the uncluttered sky, it echoes the distant peak of Triglaf, in the Julian Alps, today a small blue spot on the skyline. Pointing down to the length of white cliff underneath it, the same line indicates the great arc of cave mouth below, and lower still the white arc of waterfall where the Reka races into its swallow hole.

For S and I, Škocjan is the place where the Karst turns from a dreamscape, symbolising the good life we'll never quite have together, into a real place in limestone country, where we can pretend that we have that life. We return repeatedly. Over the years, we discover the handful of villages strung around its *doline*. Most have a church and a bus stop but little else, and none consists of more than about thirty houses. Brežec pri Divači, Gradišče pri Divači, Lezevi, Betanje, Matavun and Nakl are all in the paradoxical position of being in full sight of each other, yet not within easy reach. Houses look straight across the gorge to the washing lines and potted geraniums of life on the other side. On a still day you can hear every word when those almost-neighbours shout for their dogs or call the children in for lunch. A chainsaw in Brežec disturbs the afternoon peace of Betanje. Yet any real communication is impossible, and today these settlements are less connected than they have ever been. Apart from Škocjan, on its rocky summit flanked by the hamlets of Matavun and Betanje, they all stand at some kilometres' remove from each other, along footpaths that wind through trees and hummocks up and down and around the chasm. It takes long country miles to drive from one village to another, so hardly anyone bothers. Everyone goes into town instead: to Divača and Sežana with their bars and supermarkets, their hairdressers, pet-food shops and pizza outlets.

Yet these villagers used to be known as 'mountain goats'. Their skills as climbers and potholers were much prized. It was local men like those from the Cerkevnik family – Jožef Cerkevnik-V'ncek, Miklov France Cerkevnik, Jurij Cerkevnik-G'mboč and his sons Toni and Jože – who were key to the early discovery of the Škocjan caves, especially during the interwar years of the early twentieth century. In photos they are flamboyantly moustached, and have donned three-piece suits to pose, awkwardly, for their group portrait: countrymen not used to the assessing eye of the new.

Nimbleness is anyway quotidian in these abrupt landscapes. When everyone used footpaths to get about, the villages were as strongly connected to each other as to the outside world. The Škocjan riverbank, now uninhabited, was once busy with farms and watermills. In nineteenth-century photos the native sessile oaks, *Quercus petraea*, have been stripped out from the valley bottom. The unrecognisable foreground is bald pasture, where locals pause suspiciously, perhaps sceptically, for the camera.

Today the oaks have returned, and most of the paths leading down to the river have vanished into woodland. Only one remains, and it is right behind Jarko's house. As we descend it cautiously I notice anemones, and the wild garlic, *Allium ursinum*, which Slovenians call Bear's garlic, starring rocky ground between the trees. One April evening we found the whole path squirming with toads, the scaly brown version that is *Bufo bufo*, the common toad. They weren't just singletons on their way to the breeding grounds, but pairs already busy with the act of mating. The little males straddled their lumpen females who staggered forwards as if to get away, or as if the imperative to get to water overtook even their desire for sex.

These woods are mostly oak and hornbeam. Higher up – further inland – that changes first to beech and then to Austrian black pine, *Pinus nigra*, a huge 110,000 hectares of which were planted in the decades before the First World War in a badly thought-out attempt to reforest the Karst as quickly as possible. It's dampish under the more traditional canopy here behind Jarko's house, where the lichened tree trunks and boulders are a sign of how clean this air remains. It smells good, too. The water-saturated, greenish odour of mist and river is a reminder that, though the nearest industry at the port of Trieste is less than thirty kilometres away, it lies hundreds of metres below us ventilated by the coastal air of the Adriatic.

A single shell remains from those nineteenth-century enterprises at the *doline* bottom. The walls of an old watermill now seem set back from the river. The millrace has shrunk to a shallow trickle, between boulders where we like to sit in the evenings, watching midges flicker over the clear water. Rays of sunlight slip down the rim of the ravine. White limestone boulders gleam midstream looking as if they were made of marble.

Most of the time, though, we approach the river by the forestry track from Betanje. Iztok has been itching to show us the swimming hole, and one August afternoon he does. The water here is the turquoise of a mountain river. It runs impatiently over the bed of pebbles smoothed by its current. Close to the bank there's a single deep hollow, then a natural weir. A rope swing hangs above the pool, and a pebble beach forms a frail isthmus to protect the swimmers from the noise and drama of the white water just downstream.

S loves to swim, but he learned in the warm waters of Ohrid Lake which, though deep and glacial, are baked all summer by Greek-Albanian-Macedonian sun. Ohrid's blood temperature waters are a luxurious swim, made more sensual still by the water snakes that twine round your ankles as you work through the shallows. The River Reka is bracing: a shock even to bare feet. I roll my trousers above my knees and wade unsteadily out into a current that takes my breath away. S is dubious, poking the water's edge with a toe. His body has thickened with age, and with the steroids he takes daily to keep illness at bay, and he no longer likes to show it off.

Afterwards, though, we sun ourselves on the pebble beach. Just downstream the river bends away into the shadows cast by the trees and high banks that overhang it, then vanishes into its *ponor*, or swallow-hole, at the base of the cliff. It looks back-to-front, the earth swallowing water rather than disgorging it: and this phenomenal inversion is thought to be what drew first Copper Age, and then Bronze Age, pilgrims here.

At Tominčeva Cave, into which the water disappears, archaeologists have found artefacts dating from 3,000 years ago that seem disproportionately ritual in character. In the Great or Musja Cave, over 1,000 mainly military Bronze Age artefacts, manufactured not only locally but in the Mediterranean and in Pannonia (that great basin lying at the meeting point of Serbia, Romania and Hungary), seem to have been 'sacrificed': that is, broken, sometimes even burned, and given up to the deep chasm. It's evident that between the twelfth and eighth centuries BCE this was a place of cultic pilgrimage. Underlining this is an urn burial, large by the standards of such sites (it contains 325 graves), established in what are now orchards immediately behind where we're sitting on the riverbank. These were the graves of important figures – burials from the eleventh and tenth centuries BCE include rare iron artefacts – who, like the rich everywhere, seem to have planned on the front row in paradise.

Now Škocjan church marks this pagan site with a cross, so to speak. Its spire-topped tower rises from the tip of the peninsula round which the *doline* turns. As we saw from Iztok's viewpoint, the spot where the water disappears into the *ponor* is directly below it. Down here at the waterside, we can feel the force with which it thunders into that swallow.

The tower seems to draw sky, earth and water together into this one point. Iztok claims he feels chthonic forces at work when he stands beneath it. As we lie in the late sunlight that warms the pebbles of the riverbank, what we feel is a kind of fullness; as if the things we need in life might all, for once, have come together here.

Spring
Coleshill

Cheers!

The water blurts and splutters but I try to keep talking. You're sitting at the kitchen table, your bare elbows on the scrubbed pine. You have your sleeves rolled up as usual and I like this habit of yours, because I like your forearms. But as you talk you keep pushing at the sleeves with an impatient gesture, which I realise is unconscious and has nothing to do with appearance.

Right now you're busy telling me something. I hope this means you won't notice the way the water's splashing my shirt. Not that you'd care. But I care. I'm not unconscious of anything. In fact I'm barely listening to you, so anxious am I about the water stain on my sleeve, the peeling paint of the kitchen door, what you'll make of the muddy grass outside the window.

I force myself to concentrate. You're saying how much you'd love to go to Jerusalem. The place itself, you're saying: all those layers of settlement like sedimentary rock formation. You think it's the sort of city photos tell us almost nothing about. It's not the facades that matter, you insist, it's what's underfoot.

Water churns in the pipes above our heads and roars through the pipework beside the sink: it makes so much unnecessary noise because the pipes are furred with limescale. It's unfiltered, raw. The spring it comes from is on the hill behind the house. When I first learned this I imagined – naturally – a spring. Some trickle or gush of shining water among ferns and glittering rock. But our spring water isn't really wild. It's been captured by the landowner in a primitive holding tank. A low breezeblock wall raises a sheet of tin over a grim cement pit. In heavy rain, the runoff from the fields turns the water first orange, then brown, then into a kind of soup. When there's no rain, our water comes slower and slower. Sometimes it dries up completely. At other times, freshwater shrimps burst from the tap – they're why I never drink to the bottom of a cup.

I don't tell you about the shrimps. Instead I watch the water rush into the tumbler I'm holding. A white cloud rises from the base to meet the waterline. When it's settled there will be an egg-spoonful of limescale lying at the bottom of the glass. It's already clearing; motes of lime float in the water. I hold the glass up to the window: they look like dandruff.

I join you at the table. 'Spring water,' I announce, sliding your tumbler across. 'Ah, fantastic,' you say, raising your glass. 'Cheers!'

I raise my glass in reply, and take a swig. The water tastes sour and cool. If it were alcohol I'd call the flavour 'dry', but as it's water I can't. It is refreshing, though. Why is this, I wonder idly. Perhaps because it's not industrialised? I decide that you haven't noticed my clumsiness. This makes me feel suddenly altogether more charming and confident. 'Cheers,' I say, and I make myself look you in the eye.

Parish Map

Being a tourist is easy enough. But how do we map the localities we know really well, the ones we don't choose to explore but where we find ourselves – often with a slight sense of surprise, as if waking up from some long sleep – spending our actual lives?

The places we think of as home are a palimpsest of trivial memories and feelings. Going to the post on a particular morning, catching a certain bus, standing by that window while the kettle boils: these layered images catch us frozen in mid-gesture at the moment when for some reason they imprinted themselves.

We also understand the places where we live and work in a practical, embodied way. We're experts of distance and time, aware which end of the High Street remains in shadow throughout the short winter day, the shape particular trees assume when they're in leaf, and how long it takes to get to the last roundabout in rush-hour. We know where to buy the best coffee, or late-night milk, and which garage is always last to put up its prices. We can locate ourselves: on the weather map, in the train timetable, by the echo chamber of local accents and familiar voices. Some of this is yawningly familiar; some of it we don't even recognise we know.

And at the same time we're aware that our neighbours see even these things, these 'facts' we appear to have in common, slightly differently. Maybe that explains why so many of my neighbours in Coleshill speak of where we live as somewhere special, a physically beautiful village that has also become a special community, an eccentric paradise hiding in plain view of the North Wilts Downs, the Cotswolds, and the M4. And maybe I've simply lived here too long, or in the wrong way, and what to me feels monochrome, a used-up landscape framing the memory of former village life, truly is still more than the sum of its parts.

What I really think is that this village I know so well is less a vital, living ecosystem than a map of its own history and geography – of how it was made. In the Eighties, the British not-for-profit Common Ground started helping communities to create their own parish maps. There was something quaint and playful about this project: the maps it produced were often both highly pictorial and very discursive. It was also rather profound, juxtaposing different ways of knowing a place just as living somewhere does.

Originally, parish maps were charts of ownership. Since the word *parish* was first used in thirteenth-century English, it has been the measure of an individual church: the extent of its responsibility certainly, but also the area from which it traditionally took its 10 per cent tithe. The early nineteenth-century tithe maps that hand us down the old names of local fields were created, after all, for local taxation purposes. Today, it's hard to live within sight of the twenty-first-century Cotswolds, as Coleshill is, and remain innocent of how money maps a landscape. In the villages three and five miles away, just across the Thames, the old farm-working families have been priced out and corralled into estates on the edge of local towns: Witney, Carterton, Lechlade. They've been replaced, in the Cotswold countryside, by a genteelly aspirational monoculture of wicker-heart door ornaments and bored housewives sniffing cocaine between the school run and a trip to the gym.

Ownership imposes limits, something English hedges ('vegetable walls', as a Romanian friend calls them) have long marked out on the landscape. In a way maps limit us too. To be 'off the map' is not to count: to be mysterious, unknown, forgotten. The edge of the map is the limit of the known. And yet. To map is to unify, to draw together the disparate pieces of knowledge that make up a place. That delightful arcana of Ordnance Survey symbols – windmills, cuttings and contour lines – says, in part, there are *all these things* making up a landscape. And browsing a map is one of the most pleasurable forms of reading; a way to take an imaginary journey through a place you don't yet know.

I do know Coleshill, though; and it's a place I'm leaving, not arriving at. So it must be some quite other instinct that makes me suggest to P that we should walk the parish one last time together. We aren't quite beating the bounds, this February afternoon: not placing markers so much as taking them up, memory by memory. In the brisk, early-spring air, everything ought to feel as though it's starting. But today even the dampish, earthen tang to the wind no longer smells of possibility, but loss.

For the last seventeen years we've been living among fields and water, in a low-lying district of paddocks and prairie farms. Though this isn't quite sea level, we are at the level of the rivers that give the district its shape, and that return each spring to fill its ditches, dykes and water meadows. From the hill behind the house this shape is easy to make out. Today, as we walk the dogs along the ridge below Cuckoo Pen, we can see the whole wide, greyish level.

The February wind drums in our ears: weather here arrives from the west, and we can see what's coming miles in advance. This afternoon, high stratocumulus clouds are crowding at the horizon. There below us is our house, with its conspicuously tall stone chimney built to draw despite standing in the shadow of this hill, this limestone outlier that geologists call a *mogote*. Hill and river – in the shape of the little local Cole – together give our village its name. Coleshill. A does-what-it-says-on-the-tin toponym.

And here we are, looking down on it. There's the track behind our house that leads to Middle Leaze. There are the tin-roofed grain-dryers halfway down the track. They've been humming all winter; only now as spring comes on and they're finally empty have they fallen silent. Until last summer a couple of dozen ash trees lined this approach. Over seventeen years we watched them grow from ungainly, black-budded saplings into proper trees with bushy, rounded canopies. Then last autumn, when the estate acquired a new manager, we came back after a few days away to find that the avenue had disappeared. All that was left of it was a mess of bark chippings in the grass.

Yet Middle Leaze itself is still there: that fine old eighteenth-century farmhouse built in the local way from a mixture of brick and limestone, and slung between hipped gables. It used to be a damp, rambling hulk of a place, with flagstoned floors and a barn full of cats. Maggie lived there in a chaos of cats and chickens. An ardent, wind-tanned remnant of local gentry, she never turned an animal away. When she woke one morning to find herself covered in puppies – her latest rescue, a tiny terrier, had whelped on her counterpane in the night – she celebrated their arrival with astonishment and glee. 'But didn't she wake you?' we asked. 'Well,' said Maggie vaguely, 'I thought she was a bit restless. But then, she's had a hard life. I mean, who knows what she dreams about?'

Many of the creatures Maggie rescued at Middle Leaze got taken to church and blessed. A committed, even proselytising Catholic, she was nonetheless ecumenical when it came to her animals. High Mass, Anglican family service or Spiritualist meeting, anything would do so long as it allowed her to bring her animals to God. Eventually, of course, she was widowed and moved into her son's cottage in the village. The cats disappeared. And the weather-boarded cruck barn where so many of them had been born developed what I call Developer's Droop, the sag that is the precursor to a convenient collapse and replacement.

Wrapped in builders' tarps, Middle Leaze succumbed to eighteen months of the sort of exquisitely expensive refurbishment that aims to make it appear as if nothing has been touched. Now empty much of the year, it's become a holiday home rented from the National Trust by a City banker. At first sight it looks unchanged. The pear tree against its front wall is still a ladder of espaliered branches. But later in the year birds will help themselves to its unpicked fruit, those specially sweet freckled Williams Maggie used to leave in an honesty box at the end of the track – with the jam jar for change, if she remembered it.

From here we can pick out detail: the wavering lines of the house's lichened Cotswold stone-tile roof, the stone trim of its window surrounds, and the DPD delivery van speeding along the track. But beyond Middle Leaze the view opens out for twenty miles or more, up wide, flat valleys where the little limestone rivers of the Cotswolds meander: Churn, Leach, Coln and Dunt. Sometimes we try to spot landmarks on that plateau. Today we wonder about the pylons over to the north-west: are they the ones striding above the Churn at Bagendon? A series of towering As with straddled legs, they remind me of Stephen Spender's 'giant nude girls that have no secret' in 'The Pylons'.

'The secret of these hills was stone', his poem starts:

> ... and cottages
> Of that stone made,
> And crumbling roads
> That turned on sudden hidden villages.

Spender wrote this sometime before 1934, so it's actually wrong to imagine today's steel-girdered giants into it. His pylons are the kind of perforated concrete posts that were put up in the Twenties and Thirties. Yet the poem's insight into the secretive, just-glimpsed character of valley life doesn't date. Roads that don't run straight but wind around the contours of ridge and hollow separate places as much as they connect them.

Over there beyond Bagendon, for example, from Chedworth to Rendcomb is only about three miles as the crow flies. There's even an old straight track past the long barrow to take you there. But the tarmacked lanes make a big Z of a journey instead, tracing the ridge of the White Way then falling steeply down through the village of North Cerney to join the main Cirencester road. Through a landscape criss-crossed by straight Roman roads, and drovers' paths taking the easy route straight over the tops, the lanes winding between settlements trace river valleys we might otherwise bypass. It's the course of Sherborne Brook that joins Farmington to Sherborne and thence to the hamlet of Windrush, where it joins the Windrush River: from where lane and river wind on together into the Barringtons and on, famously, to Burford.

Every few weeks we thread our way through those lanes ourselves, on our way to meet my parents at Bagendon. Together we stroll the high ground near the pylons, across fields burred with the nutty pellets of sheep. Usually my father takes the opportunity to remind us how these bare acres were once a citadel, an *oppida*, of the pre-Roman, and then Romano-British, tribe of the Dobunni. They settled this easily managed, hospitable terrain from the Iron Age until the sixth century CE, when the Saxons ended the territorial autonomy they had enjoyed under the Romans. He points out how the *oppida*'s ditch and rampart defences are still clearly visible, especially here where beech trees line the road to Perrott's Brook.

My mother, perhaps worrying we'll be bored, often changes the subject at about this point; for example by pointing out that one of our dogs is eating sheep droppings again. She's right, but it's useless to admonish Zoi, who loves any attention. So when conversation flags, in the way of family talk, I often squint towards Coleshill and try to make out the very ridge that we're walking along now. But it's hard to spot. Rural south Gloucestershire appears oddly featureless. With its limestone roofs and well-grazed pastures of a uniform dun colour it looks undifferentiated, like somewhere nothing ever happens.

The reality's different. Our watery parish lies on the threshold of three counties, Gloucestershire, Wiltshire and Oxfordshire, and on the verge of changes we can glimpse as the lights of Swindon, the continual soughing of the M4. This afternoon, as we pick our way past Cuckoo Pen wood, we can see the acres of solar panels recently erected north of Inglesham hamlet. The consultation process for this solar farm was surprisingly brief: today, councils have targets for sustainable energy initiatives. That wasn't the case a decade ago, when five 265-feet-high wind turbines were proposed for the other side of the village. The series of planning applications that followed divided Coleshill. Those who'd bought shares in the enterprise, and those who petitioned the planning authority against it, were neighbours and in many cases also old friends. There hadn't been so much bad feeling in the community since the Affair of the Walled Garden. That was a lease-bidding war between organic vegetables and specialist historic gardening which vegetables won, though not without a certain number of prejudices surfacing: the historic gardeners were gay.

The wind farm posed altogether more complicated questions. The claim was that each 1.3 megawatt Siemens turbine, to be bought through a share issue and Co-op Bank loan, would generate the electricity to power 5,000 homes. Turbines are a renewable energy source (good), went the arguments, but carbon-costly to produce and run (bad). They don't pollute (good) but are bad for wildlife (bad). They may not be perfect (con) but if we hold out for perfection we'll never develop sustainable energy (pro). There were emotional discussions at barbeques, over fences and flowering hedges, at the open doors of cars and houses.

Cohabitation in a small community – even counting the

outliers in isolated farms and cottages, there are only 200 of us – requires high levels of compromise. The turbines marked the end of Coleshill speaking as one voice. Yet today, when you see them from the mainline trains that rush west to Bristol and Cardiff, they look like nothing so much as angels paused here to watch over us, their steel arms spread in presidential gestures.

You can't be a climate-change denier living as close as we do to the water table. There's even a trig mark on the foundation stone of our house. Our dogs have an instinct for the muddiest wallows, searching them out in tyre-tracks and ditches. Both like nothing better than to stand ham-deep in slime, lapping it up. But here on the hill things are different; drier. They have to content themselves with rabbiting under nubby hedges of elder and elm sucker.

Until the mid-twentieth century when disease arrived, Coleshill was famous for its elms. In old photos elms crowd the village green. Living under big trees makes a place seem almost supernaturally unchanging. Mature elms are especially good at this: they grow dozens of feet high and their close-packed foliage creates deep wells of shade. The Coleshill elms, specimens several hundred years old, enclosed the parish in a kind of leaf shelter. When Dutch Elm Disease, a beetle-born micro-fungus (in Britain specifically the genus *Ophiostoma novo-ulmi*), arrived in the 1960s, the National Trust worked in vain to try and rescue these great trees. They injected them with a topical pesticide and cleared surrounding vegetation that could harbour the parasite. But every elm in the parish died. Only the roots live on, throwing up series of suckers that fill the hedges with saplings, survive for fifteen years, and then succumb in turn.

Stripped of their huge, occluding canopies, this landscape becomes unignorably the level silt bed of the late-Middle Jurassic era, whose warm shallows predate human settlement by more than 160 million years. To live exposed among its flats is really to feel that geological timescale, and know how temporary human settlement is. But if our predecessors were partly sheltered from this brutal truth by elms, they also had the shelter of religion. So as we walk this high limestone spur we squint into the February wind to try and make out the tall churches of the fourteenth and fifteenth centuries – the spire of Lechlade, the tower of Fairford – that past prosperity has printed on this early spring sky.

Wool churches were built by the wealth of that mediaeval trade across the whole Cotswold sheep-rearing district. The relatively thin limestone topsoil of the Cotswold plateau is perfect for grazing sheep, who run the risk of being killed by bloat if their pasture gets too rich. In Thomas Hardy's *Far From the Madding Crowd*, the story of Gabriel Oak piercing the bloated sides of his flock after they break into a field of clover is no literary exaggeration, though puncturing the rumen might not be the first thing a farmer would do today: he's more likely to try a dose of something, perhaps bicarbonate of soda.

Mediaeval wool production was so conspicuously profitable that landowners turned entire parishes over to pasturing sheep instead of cultivating essential arable food-crops. Special longhaired, yellow-gold Cotswold Lion sheep were developed for the trade. By the time the Coleshill demesne made this change, relatively late in 1421, the wool trade – which had played a central role in generating English wealth since around 1250 – was beginning to decline. But the start it made on enclosing land – the process of ending British subsistence farming and replacing it by subsistence agricultural labour – would pave the way for the Agricultural Revolution four centuries later.

Wool churches sprout crockets and finials as if to mimic the crocketed stalactites and stalagmites that hang and climb in caves beneath their parishes' profitable wolds. By the sixteenth century, the English Reformation and the decline of the wool trade had combined to bring the heady era of their construction to an end, but the churches themselves remain. The early examples (Lechlade) are built in Early English style, the later ones (Fairford) in the Perpendicular idiom, whose flat-topped arches evoke the splayed canopies of trees.

Fairford's marvel is its mediaeval glass. Uniquely for England, St Mary's Church still has a complete set of windows. They run the doctrinal gamut from the Nativity in the north aisle to the great Doom of the west window. Not just narratively complete, the Fairford glass – with its characteristically pale-faced protagonists, whose features seem to have been inked-in by someone with a humorous eye for character – is also unique in coming from a single workshop. Barnard Flower was glazier to Henry VII and Henry VIII, and his Westminster workshop produced all twenty-eight windows between 1500 and 1517.

The result is brilliantly legible. Even today, it's easy to understand what's going on in this colourful doxology; we always bring visitors to see it. In one window in the south aisle, a beach barbeque and a crate of fish wait, with homely literalism, for the disciples who are out with Christ on the Sea of Galilee; while in the next the Ascension is portrayed as a jetpack clod of turf, with two feet resting on it as if on a footstool, at the top of the sky. Such an exceptionally complete survival doesn't occur by accident, but through proud caution and care. In 1940, the windows were dismounted and hidden for the duration of the war in the cellar of Fairford Park. In the years from 1986, they underwent a painstaking, two-decade restoration during which they were they were taken down panel by panel, cleaned, and re-leaded by specialists in York.

The dogs hate us church crawling. They resent being tied to foot-scrapers, porch gates, yew trees, the iron palings round family vaults. As we try to concentrate on Nikolaus Pevsner, tracking his I-spy of worthy architectural features in *The Buildings of England*, Dusha and Zoi raise a chorus of protest capable of penetrating both mediaeval masonry and mighty Victorian oak doors. When we emerge, it's almost always to find one or the other has wrapped her lead tightly round whatever's to hand and nearly choked herself. We constantly find ourselves apologising to strangers whose disapproval is split between They Mistreat Their Dogs (Brits) and (Americans) Those Damn Dogs Ruin It For Everybody.

But this afternoon the dogs are free to perform their zigzag survey of the rabbit warrens and deer tracks of what here is called Kings Hill. They yelp and snort, busy at their own mapping. All the while, there below us slumbers the elephant in the landscape. RAF Fairford is vast and silent. Its military demarcations, its hangars and runways, dwarf trees and churches alike.

And in this unusual inland flatness the RAF has not one but three airbases, each in a different county. Brize Norton is in Oxfordshire, over to the east and dimly visible as a series of tall end gables. Behind us, Lyneham lies south of the motorway in muddy, Wiltshire fields near Chippenham. Fairford, built in 1944 to support the D-Day Landings, is in Gloucestershire.

In 1948, Brize and Fairford were among four bases taken over by the US Airforce as European launch pads for their Cold War 'Peacemaker' B-36 bombers. The idea was that, this far inland, they could be protected by the British RAF, who would take the first brunt of any attack. It seems an astonishingly cynical calculation: but then realpolitik *is* cynical. Between 1950 and 1953, the US Air Force built a 3,046-yard runway at Fairford. At one and three-quarter miles, this was long enough to make it NASA's only designated overseas space shuttle landing site. As a result, in 1969 the airfield was picked as the British test centre for Concorde. It remains the US Air Force's only airfield for heavy bombers in Europe.

Those long shiny airbase roofs, that acreage of tarmac, are truly another country; a little piece of America right here in southern Gloucestershire. For decades it was a privileged reserve. Rumours of a fantastically well-equipped hospital abound. Some airmen only left the base to buy the salted caramel brownies the town teashop still specialises in. Fairford's little Southern Chicken shop, a Cotswold cottage set directly onto the main road, has an elderly Stars and Stripes in its window. Otherwise there's scant evidence of local fraternisation, though perhaps this is in part because the last uniformed US service personnel left in 2010. Today Fairford is just a stand-by airfield, although it still hosts an international Air Tattoo every summer.

Like wintering birds, the military planes from Fairford went mostly south, circling east of our house and climbing slowly into their long flights. In recent years the long-range bombers that were the airbase's *raison d'être* were mainly heading to Iraq. Troop carriers use RAF Brize Norton. When they fly in with a load of demob-happy servicemen and -women, on leave or finishing a tour of duty, they like to tilt dramatically as they circle the approach to Brize. Only flights carrying a repatriated body fail to make this joyous salute. Those planes tend to arrive in the middle of the day, heralded on the morning news and in the local paper. Between 2003 and 2009, as the conflict in Iraq deepened and began to seem intractable, as casualties mounted and British public opinion soured, on every occasion that a body was to be repatriated Dorothy next door came outside at the first approaching rumble, standing in silence under her clothesline to watch the plane come in. She was paying her respects. She was also trying to ward off such a fate for her adored grandson, a young army officer whose own turn to serve in Basra did eventually come. (It passed off safely.)

But in March 1999, during our first weeks here, it was B-52s that left daily, at dusk, to bomb Serbia. Dark shapes in the dark, they seemed to pull clear of the hedges only gradually, heavy laden and growling with a deep note that thrummed your teeth, shook the beams of the house itself.

Their return disturbed our sleep. We started waking before dawn. Downstairs in the half-lit kitchen, on the radio, the early news would announce what the bombers had done, to what the MoD spokesman on the BBC assured us was the industrial heartland of Slobodan Milošević's military machine. But then, later in the day, we'd see news pictures of civilians crowding the darkened bridges of Belgrade, holding their candles in nocturnal vigil. They were making a human shield round a civilian city – which the MoD assured us was not at risk. Then why this gesture, the emotion, the singing? We were left feeling uneasy. It grew increasingly hard not to hear the roar of the departing bombers as death dealing. Even the birds' evening chorus, normally so loud in March, fell silent when the planes set off. In the backwash of silence after they'd gone nothing stirred.

Less than two years later, I was being driven around Novi Sad and Belgrade in a gleaming UNHCR four-wheel drive, its tape-deck blaring fado music. I saw the pontoon replacing the main bridge that had united proudly anti-nationalist, anti-Milošević Novi Sad; saw the ruins of the hospital and the national broadcasting corporation in the heart of downtown Belgrade; saw the site of Mrs Milošević's party headquarters, just across the railway tracks from the high-rises, crowded with young families, of New Belgrade: and I understood what the vigils had been for.

Raša, the UN translator at the wheel, told me that the planes had flown so high that they could not be heard. The bombs fell from a clear sky. It seemed inconceivable. Back in Coleshill, it seemed more inconceivable still. Unbelievable that the planes that took off and landed so noisily were silent in action. More impossible still to believe that the village was connected by this web of utmost consequence to the wider world. It didn't seem real and indeed, long after the conflict in the former Yugoslavia was over, the pub continued to sell 'B-52s', stripy cocktails of coffee liqueur, Baileys and Cointreau, as if the war were nothing but a game.

Drinking a B-52 in The Radnor signified worldly acceptance of The Way Things Are, with a touch of xenophobia thrown in for good measure. Preston, local pesticide wholesaler, was always ordering B-52s. Dennis the silversmith and artist, installed at the table by the fire for his nightly omelette and chips, would roll his eyes whenever Preston entered the pub – usually on a Friday, since he didn't live in the village – drew a stool into the middle of the bar, and ordered a round at the top of his voice. A big man with a pug nose and four chins, Preston nevertheless tended to affect a cricket sweater for his Friday evening binges, as if to indicate that he could get physical if the occasion demanded it. We took him at his word – always giving him the widest possible berth – if we were joining Dennis. 'That murderer!' he would mutter into his vegetarian supper.

It's good to be outside, away from human nonsense, on this bright afternoon. Today though, we're going no further than a strip of woodland that overlooks Ashen Copse. It's February, and the village's own private snowdrop spectacular is underway. But you must climb over the post and rail by the 'No Access' sign to see it. The alkaline limestone soil here encourages snowdrops. Further north, into the heart of the Cotswolds, there are some spectacular collections. Every spring temporary car parks appear in the fields at villages like North Cerney and Colesbourne to cater for visiting galanthophiles.

Their hobby is not only narrowly seasonal; it's expensive, too. Rare bulbs change hands for hundreds of pounds. For it turns out that not every snowdrop looks the same. A rose is a rose is a rose, said Gertrude Stein, thereby revealing herself to be no gardener. I'm no gardener either, but even I can see that the common wild *Galanthus nivalis* is not the 'green' *Galanthus nivalis virescens*, with its tiny horseshoes of dark pigment on each inner tepal, which in turn is not the most common (and possibly the oldest) double snowdrop, *Galanthus nivalis* f. *pleniflorus* Flore pleno; of which the first known picture predates Carl Linnaeus's 1735 classification of the species by more than thirty years. (There's an engraving of it in *The Duchess of Beaufort's Book* of 1703.)

The green hemstitch that marks out the inner trio, and sometimes the outer trio too, of a snowdrop's tepals, the very faint, fleeting odour, something like lily of the valley, that you can detect if you get close enough, are details that repay inspection. But you have to crouch right down in the February mud to see them. For all their picturesque pallor – for all that Linnaeus named them for milk and snow – these flowers are creatures of the mud. Even their flowering is a sign that the frozen winter soil has loosened and softened again. As James Thomson rather leeringly puts it in 'Spring', 'Fair-handed Spring unbosoms every grace: / Throws out the snowdrop and the crocus first': though perhaps we shouldn't dismiss the leer, since *The Seasons*, published in 1730, was a cultural sensation which managed to inspire both Joseph Haydn and J. M. W. Turner.

I like the way the Coleshill snowdrops don't know whether they're wild or cultivated. *Galanthus nivalis* is regarded as naturalised in Britain now; but it's not *native* here as it is on the European mainland. The drifts of bulbs we're here to see, spreading for yards between the trees of this elongated little copse, were originally planted by gardeners for the Coleshill Estate – how many centuries ago? One? Two? Even three? I crouch down on the driest slope I can find to try and catch their faint perfume. The dogs wonder what's going on. They push their muzzles in my face, giving me quick interrogative licks. But what interests them more are the innumerable, much stronger odours that the February damp has loosened. Rabbit, fox, rat? We guess – and they know. As they race to and fro we have to keep calling them off the carpeting flowers: there are winter aconites, *Ernathis*, here as well as snowdrops.

Even we notice the musky, earthy variety of stinks that early spring has released in the wood. It smells of nothing so much as rot: the complex mucoid odour of fungi, the green and pissy smell of wet timber. We're used to finding the yellow brain fungus, *Tremella mesenterica*, here, and black witches' butter, *Exidia glandulosa*, which does indeed look like gobs of black ghee. This afternoon we spot the seeweedy fronds of yellow stagshorn, *Calocera viscosa*, on the old Scots pine stump near the stile. Familiar dots of colour, the bright-backed orange and black sexton beetles, *Nicrophorus vespillo*, fossick nearby for carrion among the leaf matter that gathers in the Vs of branches, on logs and on the ground.

The copse itself is fairly unprepossessing; an unimaginative mixture of run-of-the-mill deciduous trees (beech, sycamore) and small-leaved evergreens that on closer inspection turn out to be simply overgrown privet. But we know there were locust trees here too – the fast-growing workhorses of the *Gleditsia* genus, not laburnum-like *Robinia* – in the nineteenth century, because William Cobbett observes approvingly in his *Rural Rides* of 1830 that 'they are the most beautiful clumps of trees that I ever saw in my life.' And he would know. After all, it was he who had sold Viscount Folkestone all 13,600 of them.

They were planted for profit. The viscount, William Pleydell Bouverie, retired from a thirty-year career in parliament when he succeeded his father as the third Earl of Radnor in 1828. A conviction politician, he had been a Whig who voted against the Corn Laws and the suspension of *Habeas Corpus*. He spent the next forty years, until his death at the age of ninety, turning Coleshill into an Agricultural Revolutionary ideal. But it wasn't just a sophisticated food factory. He built not only a model farm but also a model estate village that included a forge, a school and community rooms – but had no pub. Every worker was given a well-constructed new cottage with a large garden and its own pigsty. It was almost a return to subsistence peasant farming; except that now the villagers grew their own food as a 'leisure' activity. The earl may have been making a profit, but he also believed that he was fighting starvation on his workers' behalf. The work at Coleshill was already underway, supplementing Folkestone's relatively liberal voting pattern, before he left parliament. After extolling the virtues of his own locust trees, Cobbett goes on to write, of a visit he made here on 6 September 1826: 'Gaunt hunger here stares no man in the face. [...] If I had to show this village off to a Yankee, I would blindfold him all the way to, and after I got him out of, the village, lest he should see the scarecrows of paupers on the road.'

Though the Agricultural Revolution shaped this landscape, the woody strip through which we're walking was planted primarily as part of a Romantic parkland. It feels like a mere curtain, nothing more than a backdrop to the downhill roll of the park south into the view. And that's probably right. It would have made Coleshill House appear as though it were at the very heart of its own landscape and not, as is in fact the case, nestled up near a local access road. Planted just inside the long park wall, these trees have never been coppiced, yet they've grown straggly and compromised by close planting. They resemble those drifts of skinny-legged, ostrich trees that the eighteenth century so loved to paint; and that we can see today in John Sell Cotman's watercolours – *Duncombe*

Park Yorkshire, or *Brignall Banks on the Greta* – or in Francis Towne's scenes from Italy.

We skirt the snowdrops. Beyond them at the shadowy heart of the copse is a dimple in the soil, a flight of earthen and wood steps and, set in the earth itself, a wooden door through whose barred grating we squint, this chilly afternoon, into a narrowing darkness. Incongruously sited near the carpet of spring flowers, it's a military bunker that has remained accessible since the Second World War, when Coleshill House and its park were used to train Auxiliary Units of countrymen; a secret army within the army.

Probably to their own surprise, the men in these Units had been picked from among the rest of the Home Guard to become guerrillas in waiting: closet heroes who would make up the British Resistance if Germany invaded Britain. Some historians object to this term 'Resistance' for the Coleshill project. They point out that the definition of such movements is that they're unofficial, arise spontaneously, and manage themselves. But I suspect that Winston Churchill, who set up the Auxiliaries in 1940, understood exactly how independent countrymen are: even casual farm labourers are used to making autonomous decisions, both day by day and in practical emergencies where livestock or workers' lives are at risk. Churchill's Units, 'seeded' by training, would quickly have become self-determining.

For the country knowledge that would have enabled them to survive and function isn't imparted 'top-down', as estate managers, no less than generals, would like to be the case. It's made by the individual himself out of his own experience. When Dorothy's husband Graham shoots the poisoned rat, his impeccable aim, with its slight anticipation of what the rat will do next, is a kind of mastery. When the contractor driving the giant Massey Fergusson perfectly aligns the furrows as they appear from under its blades, that too is the thing itself, a matter of body knowledge and practice rather than of rules.

It's maddening when what's elsewhere dignified by the term *empiricism* gets misrepresented by urban commentators as rural stupidity. But such prejudices are simply the other side of the cultural fantasy of the pastoral. As Raymond Williams – the country boy from Worcestershire who became a Cambridge don – pointed out in his 1973 study *The Country and the City,* pastoral idealises a traditional rural lifestyle which it believes has been superseded by everything urban and quotidian. Antic simplicity: it seems that these twin ideas, either counterpoised or counterpointed – rural life as perhaps profound, perhaps an idiocy, but always Other – are centuries old. Think of Touchstone, in Act 3 Scene 2 of Shakespeare's *As You Like It*, answering Corin's question, 'And how like you this shepherd's life, Master Touchstone?':

> Truly, shepherd, in respect of itself, it is a good life, but in respect that it is a shepherd's life, it is naught. In respect that it is solitary, I like it very well; but in respect that it is private, it is a very vile life. Now, in respect it is in the fields, it pleaseth me well; but in respect it is not in the court, it is tedious. As it is a spare life, look you, it fits my humour well; but as there is no more plenty in me, it goes much against my stomach.

The view from the ground differs from all of this. Paying attention to detail, whether a variation in the weather or something new going on with the local wildlife, is intelligent and practical. That such knowledge may be highly localised is no more than a form of specialisation: just so, a scholar might work on thirteenth- but not fifteenth-century legal documents, or a financial advisor have detailed knowledge of domestic but not commercial mortgages. Yet even Colonel Colin Gubbins, the officer whose extensive experience of guerilla warfare made him Churchill's choice to set up the Auxiliary Units, didn't quite understand the importance of the local. The Units trained here at Coleshill, in the very centre of the country, almost exactly as far from the sea as it's possible to be in Britain; yet the men who composed them came mostly from those coastal counties, particularly Sussex and Kent, that faced occupied France across the Channel.

Practical men, exempted from call-up by their essential 'restricted occupations', the Auxiliaries were expected to keep secret the tremendous responsibility that would have been theirs if Britain had been invaded. Rumours still surround them: that they were given just a few days' rations, because they weren't expected to live a fortnight. That in case of British defeat they were to kill the leaders of their communities – local mayors, vicars and schoolteachers, men they knew personally – who held the kind of information that would allow invaders to run the country. That they would live feral, in bunkers first modelled in the fine soil and crumbly limestone of Coleshill.

In the village itself, a similar unease continues to surround this secret in plain view. The 3,500 or so Auxiliary Unit recruits who passed through the village for training, in the months after the movement's foundation in 1940, could not have gone unnoticed, not least because at the time almost all the adults who lived in the village worked here too. Coleshill is, after all, an estate workers' village.

And it is a diagram in stone of what that relationship means. Reconstructed in Viscount Folkestone's mock-Gothic idiom of choice between 1850 and 1860, its muddily yellow cottages are built of a particularly friable limestone from the local Faringdon quarry. All mullioned windows and quizzical drip-moulds, they straggle prettily up the hill past the green, with its smashed Calvary – now just a blind stem of faceted masonry – and thirteenth-century church. At the very top of the hill Roger Pratt's mid-seventeenth-century Coleshill House stood with its back to the road (and incidentally to this copse where we stand shivering by the bunker entrance), looking instead across an apron of park to the little River Cole and the eye-catcher Castle Farm beyond.

The house was a smallish, formal masterpiece in the style of Inigo Jones, who had helped its gentleman-architect with the designs. In 1946, shortly after the requisitioned house had been returned to its owners – Molly Pleydell-Bouverie and Katherine, known as Bina, one of the great post-war British studio potters – they sold it to Ernest Cook. A grandson of the famous travel agent, Cook was a philanthropist whose name lives on in his eponymous Trust. He bequeathed Coleshill to the National Trust: but that same year, while he was still alive, it burnt down. A builder's blowtorch, left unattended, is said to have ignited beehives the family kept in the attic. Hives, combs and honey were possibly even more flammable than the old timber, lathes and furnishings of the house itself. What did the greatest damage, the story goes, was molten honey dripping from floor to floor like oil and drawing the fire down with it through the house.

The fire remains vivid in collective memory. The three engines that attended couldn't pump enough water uphill from the river to the house to douse the flames. Old photographs show a line of villagers stretching across the bottom paddock and all the way up to the house, passing buckets hand-over-hand. It could be a scene from the nineteenth century, though the year is 1952. There's an air of muted excitement, of *occasion*, to the activity. Rescued furniture stands on the front lawn as if for a rummage sale.

The *Swindon Evening Advertiser* for September 24 1952, reports: 'Villagers were visibly affected by the fire with one quote being that with the House having gone, the whole character of the village had gone.' (How consoling to discover that local journalists mangled the language even back then.) Yet something of the estate village's semi-feudal 'character' remains to this day. After the fire, the National Trust was left with a village populated by precisely the specialist workers needed to maintain such an estate. And so they kept on doing just that.

The Yard was populated with carpenters, plasterers, plumbers and electricians alongside tree surgeons, hedge-layers and dry-stone wallers. Passing, we used to hear a din of mower engines and saws revving, and the shouts and thuds and radios that mean Men at Work. There was even a foreman: a role retained until the turn of the millennium by Keith, last in that proud line, who managed to hang on long enough to be retired rather than laid off. For gradually, over the last two decades, the entire pattern of village life has changed.

It was the women, traditionally either housemaids or housewives, who were first to start working outside the village: as cleaners, or in the local supermarket. Our neighbour Dorothy did both. Then the majority of the men working at the Yard were replaced by contractors. 'Tied cottages' were 'untied' and let to the highest bidder: never a blue-collar worker. The old pattern of settling here for life has gone. Middle-class incomers fall in love with Coleshill's architectural whimsy, stay a couple of years, then move somewhere cheaper and more practical to start a family. Most residents commute to desk jobs, and the village, which now has neither a school nor a post office, empties every morning at eight.

Since he retired from the Yard, Keith's annual Guy Fawkes firework display on the Common has remained as carnivalesque and popular as ever, although the faces round the bonfire change from year to year. But it has begun to make a loss. Sometimes the pub gets too involved, turning the night into a beerfest and keeping us straggling from bar to bonfire and back. Other years it isn't involved enough, and we shiver in mizzle while Keith moves around in the darkness beyond the fire, searching drunkenly for the fireworks he's set up ahead of time. 'Fuck!' 'Where the fucksie gone?' 'Here's one now, look.'

For the heart of the village is no longer here, outdoors in the shared spaces of the Common, the Yard, the lanes and fields, but shut away among the desks of the Estate Office. Young men and women pass through the office in Stable Yard on their way to more prestigious postings. Fresh out of college, all are eager to prove themselves by squeezing money and 'use' out of an estate with no obvious jewel in its crown. Like Coleshill landowners over the centuries – the Domesday Book records Edmund of Childrey, Asgot of Hailes and Brictric of Newton as Lords of 'Coleselle' before the Conquest – the Trust is proud of its holdings, but can appear less interested in the community of villagers. The idea that a village might be a way of life as much as a *property* seems to be beside the point. And after all, modern management techniques are rarely interested in preservation.

They're more attuned to 'initiatives', such as insulating all the cottages with organic sheep's wool, or planning to turn the Iron Age earthwork above the village into a National Cycling Hub, scarred with tarmacked trails. One wise, one flagrantly destructive, what these grand ideas have in common is that neither was proposed by the people who actually live here.

It's odd, this continual process of de-authentication through which whatever's known or remembered, thought up or done by the village community itself is understood to need rectifying. It's as if the techniques of land work, whether dry-stone walling or gamekeeping, don't count as knowledge if someone has practised them all his life, but only when they're acquired by someone young and middle-class. The public schoolboy who grows his hair and chooses a holistic lifestyle as a craft-worker, and the graduate of land management courses who plans to spend his life in an estate office, are alike in being valued as 'experts'. Whereas Walter from number 17, now in his seventies and bow-legged by arthritis after a lifetime of outdoor work, is regarded as merely old-fashioned; a burden to be laid off.

In short, what remains of village life in Coleshill, as in so many places in Britain, is a hybrid form of settlement, part hamlet and part dormitory suburb: a site that (we might perversely console ourselves) has little for the tourist to see and nothing for them to do. Now that the work that was done here has been hollowed out – and I mean the school-teaching and shop-keeping as well as plumbing and harvesting, the raising of families, and even the pastoral work of the old Rectory – there's no longer any reason for the village to be here. It is just an illustration of what it once was, a diagram of how it came to be. This afternoon, as we clump briskly past the pub and the old school house, we notice again how oddly unreal the place feels. It's as if everything is just 'off': enough to create a disturbance in the balance chamber, but not for the eye to register.

Our friends Patsy and Henry believe that another reason for this feeling of oddness is a geopathic stress line running across the hill, where characteristic limestone breakages and watercourses interrupt the earth. Henry, an architect, tells us how in Germany and Austria construction sites are dowsed for these lines as part of the planning process just as, here, they would be checked for flooding or contaminants. Patsy's a wise woman whose four thriving kids and two acres of garden – all alike gorgeous and rampant – are testament to the seriousness of her beliefs. Is it she or Henry who tells us, over a glass of oxygen-rich Malbec, that cats were buried in the seventeenth-century foundations of Coleshill House to protect it against such stress?

In the etching that hangs in the pub, Pratt's House looks tall, elegant and rather like a tea caddy, as is the Inigo Jones tradition. Even Pevsner approves: 'The best Jonesian mid c17 house in England ... The staircase of Coleshill, completed in 1662, was one of the most beautiful in England.' Patsy and Henry's story about the cats reminds me of the related, darker rumour that Nicholas Hawksmoor buried a child in the foundations of some of his own early eighteenth-century masterpieces: All Souls College Oxford, Christ Church Spitalfields, St George's Bloomsbury.

Each has his signature pyramidal tower-spire, which seems loosely to associate it with the occult. Yet the very same superstitious sacrifice to the gods of place appears in, for example, the Romanian legend of Master Builder Manole. Manole has to sacrifice his pregnant wife to secure the monastery he's building in Wallachia, after he and his workers promise the mysterious force who keeps un-building their work that they'll wall up the first of their loved ones to arrive on-site if only they are allowed to complete it. It's a trace of the old religion that survives right across Europe. In Wales, the mediaeval bridge across the precipitous gorge of the River Mynach at Pontarfynach in Ceredigion is an apparently impossible feat of engineering known as Devil's Bridge. In return for building the bridge, the legend goes, Old Nick wanted the first soul across; but an old woman cheated him by throwing some food onto the bridge and tempting her cat to cross first.

Witchy, lucky and unlucky creatures, cats are so lightly disposed of by humans it's astonishing they still trust us. 'Don't sleep where cats sleep,' Patsy tells us. 'They're attracted to stressed places.' So, Henry adds, are wasps, bees and ants. Geopathic stress, he says, is the reason bees thrived in Coleshill House with such disastrous consequences.

It's hard to think of the wise and healthful bee as a signifier of environmental stress. Yet I remember the first time we stepped inside St Lawrence's Church in Lechlade. The high, wide nave and aisles, trademarks of a wool church, were flooded with light. But the floor was covered in dead bees. Dying bees hung drunkenly in the air. The building was filled with a buzzing whose note was wrong, deeper pitched than any swarm I've ever heard, as if the bees were groaning.

The volunteer sitting at the door wore a business-like anorak. 'Aren't you going to rescue the bees?' I asked her. 'It costs too much to get rid of them,' she said, not understanding my question. 'But there are beekeepers all round here looking for wild swarms.' 'Oh yes, but the church has no money.'

Shame on you. There was a special wrongness in letting these endangered, symbolic, subtle creatures starve to death in a place that's supposed to be holy. Suddenly there it was, as if it had never been away: the casual, assumptive Church in all its mediaeval cruelty.

I like bees. In summer our lawn hums not because it's especially clover-rich – it isn't: it's reclaimed field grass – but because it's perforated by ground-dwelling bees. They honeycomb the earth as if they were helping it to breathe. *Andrena cineraria,* ashy mining-bees, they're so small they look scarcely formed: the length of my middle fingernail at most. They're marked – spotted – with a dab of white and often of sky-blue on their thorax. As they hover among the daisies, no more than a centimetre above ground, they could almost be an optical illusion. The dogs are fascinated by them too; but they often eat them.

Our mining bees are solitaries, but like urbanites they are solitary in a crowd. They must find our soil attractive despite the damp: we're so low-lying that we sometimes seem to be living *below* the water table. So could there be something to this geopathic stress? I like the idea of rocks and soil becoming charged and lively in particular places. I imagine electrons swarming and seething as if in Brownian motion. Maybe, for creatures with the faculties to feel such swarming and seething, living in geopathic earth would be like using a Jacuzzi, or one of those vibrating packs that eases back pain?

I love the appreciative sound swarms make too, and the way that, once the air warms up, they scatter outriders like golden motes. We've just passed Steve's hives, set in the long grass of an unploughed headland. Now we approach a couple more, placed close to the site of Coleshill House. These aren't miraculous survivors of the fire but the remains of yet another 'initiative'. In recent years, the Trust has encouraged villagers to try beekeeping, even running skep-making workshops as if to keep us picturesquely employed.

There are, needless to say, no skeps in Coleshill. But our neighbours' own projects tend to be more durable. The ground plan of Coleshill House has been planted out in box hedges and gravel paths soft with evening primrose and other escapees from the herbaceous borders. In the February greyness it looks dimly overgrown, codified in lavender and poppy-seed heads. Beyond this rough parterre, the level site becomes a meadow that's seen service as a cricket pitch but now runs to grass which, knee-high by mid-summer, fills up with grass snakes and lost balls. It has an absolute, time-stopped feeling, like a painting by one of the Brotherhood of Ruralists. Stand here and the village is invisible. Only a sense of the Big House remains.

Denny, who planted this garden in the Seventies, lives in the Old Brew House. Her kitchen overlooking it has a high-roofed, ecclesiastical feel, though the metalled windows are small, and they're half-occluded by geraniums, stained delftware tiles, and all the clutter of a lifetime. The widow of an artist, Denny is stepmother to a tribe of architects, designers and rag-trade fashionistas who turn up in the village on high days and holidays.

When we arrive, she's sitting by a ticking Aga that's so old it seems more like a battleship than a cooker, and reading a library book through the wrong spectacles. She's wearing an Indian-print dress and her calico gardening apron, in the pockets of which are muddy secateurs and a couple of pens. Recipe books and novels, all with yellowing, handwritten notes sticking out of them, are piled on the chair next to her. A partly Persian cat, handsome but clearly a mouser, naps in a wicker chair. He's waiting for her to resume battle with the encroaching wild of the cricket field, so that he can investigate the cheese standing forgotten on the table.

It's good to be here, among the smells of ground allspice and old woodsmoke. When the tin kettle on the Aga begins to shrill, Denny gets up and spoons coffee from the Fair Trade sack on the counter into a cafetière. Outside in the flagstoned courtyard, an iron ring indicates the lid of the underground cistern that supplies her water. Her stepdaughters, now in late middle age, remember swimming as kids in its clear, shocking spring water. The tank was so deep, they tell us, that they were only allowed to swim two at a time in case they got into difficulties. In fact it's an aquifer, and if they'd swum a little further than daylight reaches they would have found themselves, like children in some fairy story, deep under the hill. *Where they would have lived forever*: the village's strange seductiveness has called two of them back to live here, as if it's something they can't quite escape.

For Coleshill's *mogote* is riddled with springs and tunnels, some natural, some manmade, and some a mixture of the two. A series of tunnels and cisterns brought water right through here to the Big House – from our spring on the far hillside. Local story has it that, after the earldom of Radnor was recreated in 1765, other tunnels allowed members of the Pleydell-Bouverie family to escape every so often from their public, upstanding life into anonymous adventure.

As we leave Denny's and make for home, we retrace our steps down a limestone ridge that is in fact lacy with hidden spaces. There's something ontologically strange about remembering that it's not straightforwardly a rock to build on. Not even a ground to stand on, though King Arthur's said to have done so a couple of miles away at Badbury, the earthwork threatened by the tarmac cycling 'hub'. A rock that isn't rocky is the agreeable, confusing paradox of limestone country.

This fundamental lack of straightforwardness, or to put it another way complexity, is a theme in W. H. Auden's well-known poem 'In Praise of Limestone'. Auden, whose native Pennine limestone country was an early touchstone, was educated among the dreaming limestone spires of Oxford and wrote his poem in May 1948 on the island of Ischia, afloat in a Mediterranean ringed by the remains of great limestone civilisations: Athens with its Acroplis *mogote*; Rome, built of local travertine and tufa; Constantinople's sedimentary basin; Alexandria, whose limestone is still widely exported; and Jerusalem.

His long, subtle poem claiming limestone landscapes for camp opens:

> If it form the one landscape that we, the inconstant ones,
> Are consistently homesick for, this is chiefly
> Because it dissolves in water.

Inconstancy, a certain playful flexibility: when we find these elements in people they charm but also exasperate us. In landscapes, too. We need the ground beneath our feet to *be* the ground beneath our feet. At first glance Auden's famous poem seems heedless of this. Metaphorical, celebratory, and very clearly not written by a poet used to getting his hands dirty, it's populated by chattering, sophisticated boys who lounge in a shady square at lunchtime, or sunbathe and flirt.

It's set in the everywhere and nowhere of symbol. Yet read it again and it's full of the special comprehension that comes from being in – from *inhabiting* – a landscape. It understands, for example, 'the local needs of valleys / Where everything can be touched or reached by walking'. Limestone, the poem gradually shows us, is a geology of subtle adjustments, a compassionate environment that allows humans to live more comfortably than we do on what it calls 'immoderate soils'.

'In Praise of Limestone' ends with a vision of heaven as a limestone landscape:

> […]when I try to imagine a faultless love
> Or the life to come, what I hear is the murmur
> Of underground streams, what I see is a limestone landscape.

They're lines that have stayed with me since I first read them. At the time I was living on the 'immoderate soils' of mid-Wales, where only a thin topsoil of mashed scree lines the mountains. That high slate country, so often rain-blackened and bare of even a scrim of yellow grass, has always been tough to settle. For this very reason it turned out to be fertile ground for religious fervour in the long nineteenth century. First came the Methodist revival of 1735, then a broader, cross-denominational one in 1859 in which up to 100,000 people are though to have converted, then the revival of 1904–5 when the same thing happened again.

Wales is a country with relatively few parish churches, but every hamlet has its chapel. Many are named for the hope of some kind of Second Coming in such desert places: Sion, Bethel. Even the villages themselves take their names from the Promised Land: Capel Sion, Nebo, Bethesda. They perch, these grim little settlements, in the kinds of landscape that Auden's 'god whose temper-tantrums are moral' might choose for His people. Theirs is a deity of the rocks and high places 'From whence cometh', according to the Psalmist, 'my salvation'. In Chapel they remember how Moses went up a mountain, Mount Sinai, to speak to God; and that later, Christ told the fisherman Simon, 'I will call you Peter, for you will be the Rock that I will build my church on': *Mae ti yw Pedr, ac ar y graig hon yr adeiladaf fy eglwys.* It's more definite in the Welsh. *Mae ti yw Pedr*, you are Peter, *ac ar y graig hon yr adeiladaf*, and on this rock I build.

Ar y graig hon. The great irony is that Caeserea Philippi, where Christ named Peter as his Rock, is nothing so absolute as a new start. Instead it's layered with compromise, as the site of pre-Christian cults of Ba'al and Pan. An exquisite conjunction of huge cave and spring nurtured those cults, for Caeserea Philippi is not 'immoderate' slate or granite – some volcanic absolute – but limestone country. The dazzling pale stone of Jerusalem is also limestone. 'Peter' is a flirt. The rock on which the Christian church is built is not muscular granite but tufa, a pale, often rather fantastical, limestone riddled with holes and with springs.

Let Auden characterise this geology:

> Mark these rounded slopes
> With their surface fragrance of thyme and, beneath,
> A secret system of caves and conduits; hear the springs
> That spurt out everywhere with a chuckle

We don't picture monotheism as built on a chuckle, that sly destabilising sound. But in the caves, declivities and runnels of limestone country, echoes bounce to and fro. We can't be sure where they originate. They confuse us. A chuckle feels like the echo of a laugh that's going on elsewhere, somewhere secret that we haven't yet gained entry to. It bounces from you to me and back again, infectious and confusing. I want to join in, but I don't want to be in its sightlines.

Coleshill's springs don't exactly chuckle. They bubble up, silenced by standing water, into the cisterns we're passing just now. Several springs puncture Kings Hill at roughly the same elevation all along this field. One makes a stream that feeds the pond next door, then runs on behind our gardens in a ditch that has become, over the years, almost invisible under fallen branches and farm waste. Another is a kind of winterbourne. In wet weather it uses the lane for streambed, and runs fanning down the tarmac to puddle in the layby opposite our house. Graham tells us that, when he and Dorothy moved here more than fifty years ago, these old houses were spongy with wet from a land drain that ran right underneath them. Sometime in the 1970s, that drain was blocked up and its stream diverted. Now our houses stay dry by floating on a bed of shingle and old terracotta pipes.

Home from our walk, the dogs shake themselves and scour their empty food bowls. The kitchen's good and warm. While they get busy muddying it, I go out into the darkening garden to bring in the washing. It hangs inert and damp on the line. Damp fills the air too, with a soft, mineral scent. Every year Graham reminds us that, 'February Fill-dyke', we'll have water to spare in these early weeks while spring is beginning, but hasn't yet officially arrived. As I haul down the sheets, I see he's left his vegetable garden half-dug because the ground is too sticky to work. He's a dim figure, picking over the last of the sprouts. I listen to his familiar, pleasurable half-singing as he mutters and hums under his breath. Then he straightens up and sees me: 'Hello m'dear.' He steps back onto the path, rocking his heels on clogs of impacted earth.

I come to the fence. Graham shakes his hoe disgustedly, 'No good. Nope.' Every year he rotates his entire crop – beans, potatoes, shallots and cabbages – apart from those summer visitors, lettuces and strawberries, which shift to a longer, gentler cycle. Carrots he eschews. They hate our limestone alkaline and develop every kind of pest. This system has worked perfectly for him for over half a century. Only in the last couple of years has the sodden earth let him down. Last year's lettuces didn't develop hearts, and his potatoes were blighted before mid-summer.

If his spuds are too small, or the shallots come up woody, Graham's routine is shaken and he grumbles up and down the garden path: another familiar, homely sound. But for him, such a broken link sends damage down into the roots of things. His life has acquired scope not through wide ambit but through deepening repetition. His 'routine' is really a kind of practice, daily as prayer or any other exercise. Living next door to him has taught me how little it matters what such practice is, *so long as you have one*. Not to be able to do such practice leaves you homeless in the world. So Graham didn't retire from gamekeeping till he was eighty, and he's a gifted exponent of all its crafts, learnt by patient, if immodest, repetition. After three-quarters of a century he makes everything he does look easy. He can sing birds out of the sky just by imitating their calls.

A couple of months from now a stray cuckoo or two, remnant of the many who gave their name to Cuckoo Pen copse a century or more ago, will pass through Coleshill, migrating north from Africa. Graham will be able to trick at least one into staying around for a few hours, just conceivably long enough for it to find itself a mate and anchor here. But we won't hear it – we'll be gone by then. 'Any news on the house?' he asks now. 'Oh, not really.' I feel ashamed, as if by moving we are giving up on a way of life. And in a way we are.

Graham and I both feel ambivalent about the cuckoo, who threatens the fragile population of songbirds but whose own old-new song is such an evocative sign first of spring and then – 'In June / I change my tune' – of summer. *Cuculidae*: even Latin can't resist onomatopoeia when it comes to this bird and its bright, fluting call. But Graham's ambivalence is unusual for him. Decades of gamekeeping mean that he divides creatures into good and bad: dogs good, cats bad. Songbirds good, raptors bad.

He particularly likes the finches and tits that set Dorothy's bird feeder swaying. Nowadays goldfinches, *Carduelis carduelis*, are turning up more and more often. Their glamour comes most of all from the flare of red around their beaks. The little yellowish siskins, *Carduelis spinus*, call in only when the weather's bad. They're the shyest feeders on the wire holder. Round here it's the great tits and long-tailed tits who dominate among the *Aegithalidae*: robust, gregarious country-dwellers. Graham also watches out for the small seasonal visitors – wagtails and skylarks, flycatchers and redstarts – who raid the fields around us for chaff and insects. He can summon up robins with fighting talk, whistling their territorial calls; but robins are the familiars of every garden. More impressive are his fluent thrush song, and the shy wrens he coaxes into view. But magpies, those unlucky birds, he regards as vermin because they eat the eggs of favoured species. The pheasants and partridges on these estates can barely be described as ground nesting, since they're mostly incubated by gamekeepers: Graham himself used to breed hundreds every year. But many of the songbirds he enjoys most – the ground-nesting skylarks and hedge-nesting thrushes in particular – are vulnerable to magpies and other predators.

When we first moved here Graham kept two magpies in a Larsen trap. From its mesh cage the trapped birds uttered their distress cry, luring others near enough to be caught or shot. When they weren't being put to work like this, the magpies and their box lived on top of the woodpile behind his tool shed. All day long they hopped between two perches, alternately next to each other then apart. On the day that Graham retired from Coleshill shoot the magpies disappeared – and they were not set free. If Graham spots magpies nesting in the trees that line the paddock, he strolls down the lane, takes aim and brings them down. I've often met him coming back with a bird dangling from his arm. We stop to talk – about the weather, or his new car – and all the while the dead bird dangles there, surprisingly large, its white chest bosomy and firm. The wrinkled eyelids always seem closed in disgust rather than pain. As we talk I keep glancing down, expecting them to fly open.

But Graham has no difficulty handling dead or dying creatures. He'll hang the magpie on the trophy wall of his chicken run, which in his prime was festooned with the dried-out corpses of rats, stoats and mice. He believes it serves as a warning to other 'bad' creatures like rats – and foxes, which Graham particularly hates because he believes they kill for sport. Once, decades ago, a fox got in his chicken run and killed every bird in it – but made, he says, no attempt to eat a single one. 'Never a one. T'was just for the enjoyment.'

It's ironic hearing an attack on killing as sport from a gamekeeper – and anthropomorphises foxy instinct, too. But Graham's fond of his chickens. I like hearing him chat to them every morning, as he tosses them the contents of the kitchen compost bucket: 'Ah, you like that, don't you, you like that.' Most of the year now their run's nothing but mud, and the grumpy birds peck at each other till the weakest ones are bald and bloody; but I remember when grass still grew back within the wire walls each spring. Graham used to keep a second flock, and a second cockerel, in the pheasant-rearing paddock. The two cocks would wake us at four every morning. Their duelling braggadocio was funny in our first week in the house, tedious by the end of the first month, and a cause of chronic sleep deprivation by mid-summer.

The paddock hens would get broody and wander off to sit about under hedges. One soft-feathered Rhode Island Red made her home in our dry ditch for several weeks. When she abandoned the nest, she left behind two unhatched eggs, which I put in our airing cupboard. One hatched. Perhaps he was a cock: he certainly woke us with piercing peeps at three a.m. I spent the pre-dawn feeding him drops of Rescue Remedy, until at first light Graham showed up and claimed custody, carrying the chick off in his fist: *how did he know?*

Bantams try harder to escape than hens do. Some manage a fluttering leap onto the high fence of the run. Whenever he notices, Graham clips their flight feathers. He has a little sentiment when it comes to poultry, but not too much. Recidivist bantams, and hens who get too old for laying, have their necks pulled in a corner of the run. A sound of flurrying wings and a stutter of clucks. They're for the pot.

Cue the Sunday lunchtime surge of the extractor fan, recently wished on Graham and Dorothy by the National Trust when their cottage was renovated. It's not without attendant anxieties. Proper country people don't open downstairs windows, but prefer to conserve warmth and the good smells of cooking. So the fan goes on for little more then ten minutes; just enough to disseminate those appetising aromas around the garden.

And yet Graham's whole family sleep with their bedroom windows open. This must surely be a kind of modesty, fresh air dispelling the intimate odours of sleep, for it's certainly not practical. Once these waterlands warm up, come May, our night-time windows let in the crane flies and mosquitos whose squashed bodies star our bedroom ceilings, and who get their revenge by biting us.

But craneflies, *Tipulidae*, horrify me with their tendency to lose their fragile, hair-like legs yet keep on – what exactly is that movement? Bouncing – and cricking against walls and window, and in my hair. Scientists call the special ease with which they lose their legs *deciduous*, so maybe they feel no pain. All the same, their indefatigability is itself hideous, like the indestructibility of cockroaches or the way worms wriggle away when you accidently sever them with a spade. Cranefly larvae are just as repellent: those 'leatherjackets' we find in our compost and on the banks of ditches, strangely elongated and often with heads retracted into what looks like nothing so much as a foreskin.

Moths come in at our open windows, too. Duncan has dropped in for coffee, and as I fill the percolator we chat about what he's seen recently. Among the most common moths here is the angle shades, *Phlogophora meticulosa*, in its camouflage fatigues, and the dusty, rather tired and ripped-looking yellow shell, *Camptogramma bilineata*. We also have lots of small magpies, *Eurrhypara hortulata*, with their neat brown borders. The lovely, vivid rose-scarlet cinnabar, *Tyria jacobaeae*, appears surprisingly often on the windowsill too.

Duncan's paintings, their foregrounds crammed with giant four-petalled rape flowers, are an appeal for biodiversity and for attention to the shrinking countryside. As well as being an artist, he's the village lepidopterist. Sometimes he'll disappear on a long tramp, venturing into copses far off the beaten track and down the concealed banks of ditches where he records rarities like the marsh fritillary, *Euphydryas aurinia*, and once or twice a purple emperor, *Apatura iris*. ('Auriana', 'Apatura': the Latin names swirl like draperies in a painting by Tintoretto or Titian.) Lacking a pupil or protégé among his own kids, Duncan writes up his finds as 'Nature Notes' in the one-sheet village newsletter. This afternoon, over our coffee, he tells me how here in west Oxfordshire, despite conservation initiatives we're still losing the wall brown, *Lasiommata megera*, and even the grayling, *Hipparchia semele*.

I listen and nod, and I do care. But I'm also guiltily aware that, rare or not, all these window-hopping moths and mosquitos feed the bats who nest in our attic, and who are one of our great delights. Their swooping corner-of-the-eye flight is one sign that spring has arrived at last. Ours are soprano pipistrelles, *Pipistrellus pygmaeus*, whose high-pitched echolocation we can just occasionally hear as they flicker and jerk in the evening air above us. I like to sit on the bench outside the back door, not doing much, just keeping them company as they forage and snack: this eating at dusk seems somehow both scrutable and sociable.

It must be a dozen years now since visiting 'experts' tried to map the village sites where bats roost, but failed to explore the attics of private houses. Instead – or so local gossip goes – they tried to ban the ringing of our church bells. None of us can quite remember whether any bats were actually rescued from our proverbial – if actual – belfry. Was this something we saw on the telly? Or did it truly happen here, one day when we were out at work perhaps? All we know is that the six bells still ring – whenever a team of ringers can be found, that is. Thursday evening is practice night, when the 'all's well' sound of peals streams thinly over the hill to us.

We rarely have experienced ringers, so the sound itself is all arrhythmic clotting and bunching. When two bells accidentally sound at the same time the whole air buzzes. It must be deafening in the tower itself. 'Tenor: 7cwt in Bb', the Diocesan Guild of Church Bell Ringers records. Possibly this is why a full set of changes has been rung only five times since we've lived here. *Felstead Database* lists them all: 'Surprise Minor (7 methods) – 4th November 2002; Spliced Minor (14 methods) – 20th February 2011; Minor (7 methods) – 2nd August 2012; Minor (5 methods) – 26th April 2013; Plain Bob Doubles – 8th March 2015.'

The tower's thirteenth-century masonry remains astonishingly unshaken. Its features have been blurred by time though, and by the iconoclasts who during the English Civil War destroyed every religious image – every *graven* image, they would say – that they could reach. Sometime between 1642 and 1651, the corbels lining the south aisle of St Michael and All Angels disappeared. All that remain are three gargoyle monsters who lean from the drip mould that forms a cincture round the tower.

So many saints and angels disappeared in this way. John Ruskin concluded, when he came to write 'The Nature of

Gothic' in 1853, that the mediaeval mind was 'savage'. To him this was a positive quality, denoting imaginative spontaneity. The shock troops of Oliver Cromwell's New Model Army were less approving. They took the Biblical prohibition against idolatry, in Exodus 20:4, as an excuse for gleeful vandalism: 'Thou shalt not make unto thee any graven image, or any likeness *of any thing* that *is* in heaven above, or that *is* in the earth beneath, or that *is* in the water under the earth.'

Today, this district of fields and water at the dead centre of England and Wales is comfortably unimportant; left behind by urgencies of realpolitik that only the local airbases still connect us to. Perhaps, too, it's a little exhausted. For this hasn't always been the case. To the west of this region of hill forts standing in the sightlines of the Uffington White Horse – symbol of a lost Bronze Age belief system – stands Malmesbury: first capital of all England and where Aethelstan, England's first king, was buried in 939. During the English Civil Wars this region changed hands often, and so saw more fighting than did either Royalist or Parliamentarian strongholds; we're ringed by the sites of decisive battles. The Royalist defeat at the Battle of Stow-on-the-Wold (1646) was the end of the first Civil War. At Worcester in 1651, the Parliamentarians ended what had started, just two miles to the south of the same city, nine years earlier. In 1649, soldiers of the New Model Army mutinied at Banbury. In that same year, Oliver Cromwell rounded up 340 Levellers, the radical political idealists who fought with his Army but had come to see him not as a social liberator rather as a religious dictator, imprisoned them in Burford Church, and shot three of their leaders in its churchyard.

Yet here's Coleshill today with what I think of as its picture-postcard looks. The church is built from local, greyish-yellow limestone. This is not the discreet grey of Gloucestershire's Lower Jurassic limestones, the Lower and Middle Lias that runs along the Cotswold edge above the Severn, with its patches of Cotteswold Sands and Inferior Oolite. Nor is it the heavy gold-ochre of North Oxfordshire's Upper Jurassic, where that county stretches towards the sandstone and clay of Northamptonshire and Warwickshire. It's not even the honey glaze that limestone acquires in the post-glacial valleys of the Windrush and the Coln, at Burford or at Bibury. No, this is the workhorse Middle Jurassic, the Callovian sediment that slides under the later chalk of the Berkshire and North Wiltshire Downs and down deeper still, down to depths of six, seven, eight hundred metres, under the London clay.

It's easier to trace this on maps spread out on the kitchen table than it is standing outdoors in the landscape itself. I unfold the brightly coloured British Geological Survey 1:250,000 sheets, borrowing Duncan's coffee mug as a paperweight. This region of some hundred square miles reaches from Gloucestershire in the west, south into Wiltshire and east to Oxfordshire. It straggles up from the muddier tracts of Wiltshire – from Melksham, Trowbridge, and even the tip of Somerset around Bruton – to slip into Gloucestershire by the back door, north of Swindon. Here, farm cottages and modern villas make up the quietly busy community of Down Ampney. With its wide lanes and large horse chestnut trees, the village has an air of settled decency. It seems to deserve the hymn tune that the composer Ralph Vaughan Williams, who was born here, named for it.

Onward past the sugar bowl, our district stretches to Meysey Hampton, all poplar and willow, and south to Castle Eaton in Wiltshire, where Dave the mechanic sleeps above the scrap in his barn workshop, surrounded by a quarrel of half-wild cats. Turn left at the milk jug. Now this territory briefly becomes the Cotswold Water Park, which seems to be not so much a geophysical spot as a gated resort for second homes and sail-boarding, then eastward again mixes with the Thameside water meadows at Lechlade. Further east, and as we near the edge of the table it turns into Oxfordshire: at Kelmscott, Clanfield and on to Bampton and Brize Norton.

It's a district that is no-district; not Cotswold, not Vale. Even the local oolitic limestone itself is deprecating. Newly split, it's beautifully pale. But once it's exposed to the air it quickly dulls to a muddy grey caused by sulphation, a reaction between sulphur dioxide in the air and the calcium carbonate of the stone. Millions of minute fossils are coated with lime to create the equally minute 'eggs' that give this stone its name: from *olio*, the Greek for egg. So, though technically a freestone which can be cut and dressed at will, it betrays its desire to split into layers in the ragged edges of its dry-stone walls.

Still, the stones ploughed up in the fields spring after spring are gleaming and white. On the chestnut-coloured soil they appear incongruous, like rubbish or the fists of frozen snow that line its furrows after a thaw. And almost every chunk contains fossil seashells. These include scallops and clams, immediately recognisable across the millennia. There are also pipe-like forms that seem related to razor shells and to coral itself, and dimpled fossil sponges that look like poured concrete.

Oolitic limestone is loosely packed and spongy with the billions of fossils that were never compressed by subsequent geological events, but appear simply to have hardened together, and that evoke the warm, shallow seabed in which this landscape was laid down roughly 160 million years ago.

Deep archaeology. I find myself thinking about Pannonia, the inland sea that in the Miocene and Pliocene – that is, between 23 million and 2.6 million years ago – created the wide flatlands of northern Serbia, western Romania and southern Hungary that curve on to Slovakia and Croatia. Geological time is incomprehensibly grander than human history. Pannonia, though geological fact, feels like a legend.

Closer in both time and space, Cantre'r Gwaelod – the legend of a fertile land that filled Cardigan Bay until its sea defences were left unattended – finds an echo if not proof in the fossilised forests among the real sands of Ynyslas, or 'Silver Island', whose peaty stumps appear at low tide. The fossils I have always picked up and discarded when we walk our local fields in spring are like nothing so much as rumours, hints of a radical past in which countries rose from the water and fell back into it.

Nature isn't unchanging but changeable; and at the moment it's changing here very fast. Graham, coming into the kitchen now with his spare key, pauses to have a mug of tea with us, and tell Duncan how these fields used to fill with curlew. In seventeen years here I've never heard a curlew skirl. But until two years ago peewits always nested here, and in parkland on the other side of the hill. I was astonished when I first heard their electric cry, in fact I assumed it *was* some sort of electronic device. Something to do with the airbase, I vaguely thought.

It was our first March. The cry that carried on the sharp east wind was sharply space-age, and it scoped up a major sixth – unexpected interval. Peewits also make a *vibrato* sound, a bit like a flute when it's flutter-tongued. If their uncanny, *pheeeeeewit!* call is unmistakeable, so is their flight. Especially when mating, or feinting to see off predators, they alternate steep climbs with abrupt downward collapses. The ascents are smooth but the descents are broken-winged, *lapwinged* indeed, toppling alternately one way then the other. It's an utterly plausible mimicry of casualty, at least the first few times you see it.

Close up, the speed and asymmetry of this fall are urgent with alarm. Walking the track to Middle Leaze, we used to startle nesting birds. They'd leap up from their unseen eggs as if catapulted out of the ground itself, only to dive over our heads: the abrupt tumbles becoming threateningly fast swoops. The black markings of the outer half of their spatulate wings, and the white feathers of the rest, flash alternately when lapwings dive: like a flicker-book, like go-faster stripes. Our old collie Juno was terrified.

Now Juno's buried under the willow, and the fields at Middle Leaze are silent each spring. Graham remembers huge flocks of lapwings, like the ones we saw one bitter January day in the fields behind Old Sarum. By the time we came to live here only five or six breeding pairs returned each year. Then only two. Three or four springs ago a last lapwing rose and flopped in pointless, solo dance.

You don't have to be a country genius to work out why. Year in year out, despite the fact that this is National Trust land, the estate ploughed these fields within a couple of weeks of the birds nesting. The only reason lapwings survived here as long as they did was that some had the stamina to start over with a second brood. Meanwhile every Easter the farmer on the other side of the village would let his cattle out onto the grass and straight across the defenceless nests. Later in the season he'd move the stock, let the grass grow, and mow in time to pick off any second brood.

Basic nature conservancy puts a rope fence around the relatively small patches of ground where birds do nest; such basic practice is what donors might imagine they pay conservation charities like the National Trust for. But round here wealthy estate farmers, who run thousands of acres and employ contractors to provide the hands-on dirty work, expect to do with the countryside pretty much as they wish no matter who their landlord is.

Graham, though, blames not gentleman farmers but badgers and raptors for the disappearance of our ground-nesting birds. This is a favourite topic, and while the kettle boils he warms to it. We're on the edge of a district where badgers have been culled as an experiment in managing bovine tuberculosis. Graham, though, dislikes badgers for other reasons. To him they're savage, dangerous beasts, something like small bears. In the warm nights of our first summer here, he often warned us against walking past the sett in the lane. 'They'll go for your ankles,' he told us solemnly. 'You need leather gaiters if you're goin' up there.' In all the years since, we've only ever seen one badger there.

Not so savage, then. Just once, walking the Middle Leaze track with Juno, I heard a strange grunting and barking and a young badger, not yet full grown, shot out of the ditch in front of us, followed almost immediately by a second. Furious and furiously absorbed, the two creatures rolled over and over, struggling and snorting. They were right at our feet for maybe ten minutes during which Juno, as astonished and impressed as I was, made not a move: suddenly they rolled together into the ditch and disappeared.

Graham maintains that badgers eat the eggs of ground-nesting birds. So they do. But from their sett in the lane they'd have to cover a good quarter-mile across open ground to reach the old nest site at Middle Leaze. However sturdy and rapacious a dog badger may be, he's a short-legged creature in a landscape peopled by his human predators and, I find myself arguing as I pour the tea, can never be as comprehensively destructive as a Massey Ferguson. When Graham switches to arguing that it's raptors who consume the eggs and chicks of ground-nesting birds we agree again, and this time it's Duncan who steps in to argue that a single hungry beak makes slow work of what a giant tyre can obliterate in less than a second.

I pass the biscuits round. Graham is, in his own way, a kind of birder. The shoot he spent most of his life working for was a farmers' syndicate, run on a shoestring. He managed it single-handed. In return, when he reached state retirement age the farmers sacked him, 'untied' his cottage from the job, and took him on again at the same wage – and with his own rent to pay. For decades he worked seven days a week, every week of the year, hand-rearing the shoot's hundreds of pullets from eggs he incubated in the family's own dark back kitchen. In the Eighties, Nineties and Noughties, when other gamekeepers rode off-road trikes from feeding site to feeding site, he carried a heavy sack of meal himself, tramping the acres of the estate on foot. He spent Sunday afternoons mowing the two-acre rearing paddock by hand. When the syndicate retired him a second time, at seventy-five, he went to work for his son, who keepers on a neighbouring estate.

As Graham reminisces, Duncan is getting ready to leave. The windows have darkened. Hedges and trees have become almost indistinguishable from the sky; only the dim gold glow of Swindon's polluting lights differentiates the top from the bottom of each pane.

When the hedge opposite was last laid, about five years ago, several saplings were left to become full-grown ash trees. Now, thirty or more feet high and shaggy with last year's keys, they make perfect perches for migrants; fieldfares, redwings, waxwings and starlings. All winter and well on into spring these fields are visited by flocks of between a dozen and a hundred birds at a time, scattering across the landscape like scraps blown in on the wind.

This evening, as I open the front door for Graham and Duncan, I notice some twenty or thirty fieldfares, *Turdus pilaris*. I can tell them by their reddish-brown wings and speckled chest markings, not so different from those of a mistle thrush. Like redwings and waxwings, they *are* members of the thrush family, of course. And these birds flying down into the rye and up again into the ash trees probably summered in Scandinavia. They're used to this thinnish northern light, to this cold, early spring wind. Some of our migrants come all the way from Siberia, after all: an effort that seems as prodigal as it is prodigious, and a salutary reminder of how far north we truly are – since, while we're at a latitude of 51.72 degrees, the capital of Siberia, Novosibirsk, is a mere 55 degrees north, and Vladivostok a southerly 43.2 degrees. Migration seems such a crude natural mechanism, I say; and Duncan, pulling on his boots, agrees. Even Graham bobs his head without disagreeing.

As both men leave, I wonder whether it's for the last time. I take a final look over their shoulders. It's cold tonight: the last few mornings we've woken to glorious hoar frosts. A skein of geese oar overhead, calling in chorus their imitations of our goodnights. They're returning to their lakeside roosts, as they do every evening at dusk. Disturbed by the geese or by the light from the doorway, the fieldfares rise together from the hedge and scatter into the next field.

I shut the front door and, followed by the dogs, go from room to room drawing the curtains, as if I were closing down the chill outdoors. In fact, out there in the darkening landscape, everything's just starting up. Another month or so and the house martins, *Delichon urbicum*, will be back; the trees coming into leaf. Soon it will be April, when almost everywhere manages some good looks; Coleshill is no exception. Verges and pastures are transformed by cow parsley, the wild and the orchard apple and plum and the sombre early pear come into blossom. The first voices sound in the village gardens. Cricket starts up on the top field.

Tonight though, only the barn owl from Middle Leaze is visibly in possession, working her way across the paddock. She maps her hunting ground methodically, up and down over the dark acres as if she were drawing a plough through the air. It's not so bad, after all, to know that she'll still be here when we are gone.

Winter
Jerusalem

Ah!

At dawn, all over the city, flames seethe and hiss under coffee pots. In the narrow streets of the Old City, in the concrete blocks that straggle from it in all directions, in dark back kitchens and smart studio apartments, in the cubby holes of concierges and on braziers outside army checkpoints, in living rooms, at family breakfasts, on ancient one-ring stoves balanced between orange boxes, water and ground coffee begin to wake up to each other. The hippie students in their rainbow-coloured campervan measure out sweet Ethopian ground with a teaspoon. The old Russian in the top floor left, where a smell of borscht lingers on the landing day and night, fiddles with trembling fingers at the top of the percolator, which his daughter screwed too tight when she was here yesterday. In the bedroom his dreaming wife smells the odour of the neighbours' coffee that comes floating through the open window, and turns over with a snore. Two cafés haul up their shutters at almost the same moment, and their rival owners step out to view the morning street, while in the dark interiors behind them the Gaggia machines snort and wheeze through their morning steam-clean. At the kiosk where half the city buys its cigarettes Tamara, fiercely painted and nobody's fool, drinks her takeaway coffee from a paper cup, grimacing and cursing at the awful taste. Across the dormitory suburbs wives are filling percolators, spooning in the Costa Rica Special, lighting the gas, shouting for lazy teenagers to get out of bed. Art experts in elegant dressing gowns tip chunky beans into brass mills and, as they grind, the sweet heady smell of coffee rises into the air and seems to slip via their nostrils directly into their brains until they feel their minds opening like the flowers placed in large glass bowls on their breakfast bars. Schoolboys with dirty fingernails tip enamel coffee pots glumly towards their breakfast bowls. At the entrance to the souk where the other half of the city gets its cigarettes, Omar leans against a window ledge to watch the world go by while he sips from a coffee cup he holds delicately, with both hands. Half awake, wives in the east of the city stir the fine coffee-dust in their ibriks, watching it mix with the heating water into a silky brown that they let come to the boil, then take off the heat, then boil again. Three times the smooth thick mixture rises to the rim and sinks again as they stir. In brass and steel and enamel pots, sometimes with cardamom seeds floating on its surface, with and without a gritty admixture of sugar, the morning coffee rises and falls and rises before it splashes into the waiting cups. In the breakfast rooms of high-rise hotels, American tourists and journalists in creased chinos help themselves to reheated coffee that tastes of chicory. Coffee cups clash and clink in the kitchens of the government buildings. The runner at the TV studio burns his fingers on the plastic cup of coffee he's fetched for the celebrity who will be interviewed straight after the headlines. Factory security guards loosen the tops of thermos flasks with a sigh of satisfaction and the knowledge that the night shift is nearly over. And from every part of the most infamous city in the world, with a chorus of clinking and chinking, of yawns and grumbles and farts, with the hoarse hissing of taps and gas flames and slopping of black liquid into cups, the smell of coffee rises into the pearly morning air like incense, like prayer, like hope and hangs there, an almost visible haze, grown almost pinkish now in the colours of dawn, as the waking city – that has not quite remembered yet what it is or what it has to be worried about – exhales, *Ah!*

Unreal City

Sì lunga tratta
di gente ch'i' non averei creduto
che morte tanta n'avesse disfatta

'Such a long line / of people that I would not have thought / that death could have unmade so many,' says Dante Alghieri of the damned, in his *Inferno*. Six centuries later, Dante's doomed dead turn revenant in *The Waste Land*, T. S. Eliot's vision of rush-hour commuters in 1920s London.

We make places our own in part by the stories we dream up about them; and not all of those stories are idylls. Writing seven decades before *The Waste Land*, Charles Baudelaire transformed 1850s Paris into an 'Anthill city, city full of dreams, / Where the ghostly accosts the passer-by in broad daylight': lines, from *Les Fleurs du mal*, that would also later come to haunt Eliot's London wasteland. We pass these dreams about places to and fro, borrowing and evoking them as if our reactions were reality and the geophysical given something unreal, endlessly open to being reshaped.

Daydream and memory can be elegiac, covetous, even visionary – as when they lead to the creation of a model village. Nowhere are they layered more densely than in cities, where 'neighbourhood' may mean not community but simply proximity, and where the impossibility of 'slow knowledge' – that prerogative of country living – means that the whole place never quite fully reveals itself.

However hard pastoral works to create a repository for nostalgic sentiment, the fundamentally incomprehensible urban environment is always more of a dreamscape than countryside could ever be. Longed for and feared, its streets paved with gold, the Great Wen of human corruption: the city whispers to us in our sleep. Yet these personal temptations are innocent compared to the dreams and nightmares that whole societies entertain. Those fantasies devour the places they fix on through colonial exploitation, through war and plunder, even through mass tourism. Every city is as much unreal as real. But it's the most dreamt-of places that are the most tragic.

To get to Jerusalem you have to pass through the Valley of the Shadow of Death. At least that's what it feels like at the airport. Check-in for El Al and for South African Airways is isolated at the far end of the departures hall, away from customers flying to safer, more neutral destinations. To walk the length of that empty hall is already to feel exposed.

Things don't get much better when you join the little group of your fellow travellers in the cordoned area by the gates. You're repeatedly asked the purpose of your visit and where you'll be staying. The questioning isn't aggressive, but it is forensic. You understand that this stuff matters. I queue behind a group of elderly Londoners from the East End. As their baggage is unpacked and sifted, they grumble. 'Oh come *on*.' 'It's obvious we're no threat.' In fact, I doubt it *is* obvious to the young Israeli in her tight-fitting security uniform, who marshals us like a faintly impatient captain of netball. She is absolutely unable to recognise an East End accent; even if she could, it's likely that she wouldn't know what that signifies in Jewish diaspora history. And she would distrust her assumptions anyway, because that's the logic of safety.

For these kvetching elders who must have lived through the Nazi era as kids though, going to Jerusalem is not a matter of logic but of the heart, and what they *feel* is that they have been rejected by the city where they dream of belonging. They've probably supported the country we're on our way to all their lives, year in year out, collecting tin by collecting tin and charity concert after charity concert. For many in their generation it will have been a cause, hope, something they felt they could take part in to make a difference: an answer to Hitler, and a story of survival. Not the problematic, actual, modern state of Israel, brutalising its minorities and founded on a New World model of displacement. Their dream is of somewhere altogether more ideal. This land of milk and honey probably has a planned economy. It is likely constructed on the same 'blank space' that the Americas, Canada, Australia and New Zealand imagine themselves to occupy. The kibbutzim peopling this imaginary country are polymaths, outdoor intellectuals who can grow oranges in the morning and win Nobel Prizes for Chemistry in the afternoon. They are all-shall-be-equal peaceniks who want to create a new state through up-to-date agricultural management, 'greening the desert' and a highly developed tourist industry built on the beaches of a sunny paradise.

These grumpy Londoners with their out-of-date suitcases – no wheels – and zip-up leisure gear are on their way not to the tangle of challenges that is Israel or Palestine, but to the Jerusalem of their imagination. But aren't we all? Though there are other sites that are as holy or holier to yet greater numbers of people – Mecca, the Ganges – Jerusalem *is* after all arguably the most famous city in the world. Those who dream about it dream deeply, as they have since the First Crusade in 1095–9, or the Roman Siege of Jerusalem in 70 CE, or six centuries BCE when Nebuchadnezzar captured the city.

So as the plane circles and starts its descent to Ben Gurion airport, I'm overwhelmed by a sense of how extraordinary it is to be doing this. Those twenty-first-century lights below us, those dimly glimpsed buildings, are the city that so many famous people through the millennia have imagined, and for every George Frideric Handel or Michelangelo there are the anonymous or forgotten millions. But it's I who get to visit. For a moment I feel special, even 'chosen'. But then, '*Mazel tov!*' says the pilot over the intercom, and you might wish he'd tell us everything is in hand rather than wish us luck. Perhaps this is why applause breaks out all along the aisle when the wheels touch down; or perhaps landing here *is* special.

Matchboxes and ping-pong balls, eggshells and tissues, felt pens and the heady smell of Copydex as it stuck to your fingers in white webs. In Llanbadarn Church Hall we laboured over the sheets of beige, purple and grey sugar paper on which we were constructing our Jerusalems. Gas heaters fizzed above our heads and rain streaked the windows. The long Sunday mornings droned by as we moved slowly about our business at the trestle tables. However they sold it to us, Sunday School was really just an excuse for an extra half day in the classroom. The metal-and-canvas Church Hall chairs knocked our knees and shins when we fidgeted or tried to kneel up on them. Sometimes Mandy had a fit, sliding awkwardly off her chair and, for a few minutes, out of reach. Sometimes Christopher played up crazily, pushing the stacks of chairs around and shouting. We took little notice. We spent all week together anyway, at proper school.

Besides, we were veterans of glue and paintbrushes. We knew how to screw a pencil-sharpener to the side of a table, how to revive a dried-up felt pen with spit, how to slice a portion of sugar paper from the heavy roll using only one blade of the scissors. We'd done it all before for Bethlehem and for Nazareth. Now it was Jerusalem's turn. We understood the mysteries of collage and of bas-relief, and were only too happy to abandon the concentration that proper models demand for the easier option of 3-D pictures. To represent flagstones, we crushed eggshells and glued the resulting fragments along the paths we'd drawn. We took the blank inner drawers of matchboxes and fixed them with hinges of Sellotape to make the flat-roofed box houses of the Holy Land. In times of plenty, we wrapped them in notepaper so they would be white like the houses in the Jesus picture books.

The sky was blue. This took a lot of determined felt-penning, and was heavy on resources. After we'd used up the best colours in the pen tray, we'd experiment with navy or turquoise skies. But even at the start of every year, with a perfect pack of new felt tips, it seemed like make-believe, and so porous was the sugar paper that the colouring-in was usually stripy. Our own sky was never anything but grey. Colouring it blue was what the grownups told you to do but a blue sky was no more real than the place they called The Holy Land.

Still, we stuck drifts of cotton wool onto the coloured-in sky to make clouds, and clamoured for the carefully halved ping-pong balls that were handed out to make our domes. In memory, it seems as though neither we nor the mothers who ran the Sunday School were able to work out that the balls needed to be *quartered* to work in bas-relief. Or maybe we just didn't care. Our collages began to curl at the edges before we'd even finished work on them, and those with less carefully cleaned eggshells developed a curious sulphurous odour. When church was finally over we couldn't wait to get home for Sunday dinner, potatoes and frozen peas and hot grey meat. Jerusalem waited the week out, forgotten in the boot of Mrs Jackson's car.

Blue sky above a limestone landscape: the old northerners' dream of the south. The stone looks as pale as if the sun had bleached out all the pigment, and the sky is such an absolute blue that you don't know what to do with it. Should you drink it or lick it?

In this version limestone country smells of coconut-scented sunscreen and the sour citrus of insect repellent. To some visitors the heat is dazzling, hallucinatory. The sharply white limestone, the smells of diesel and cooking oil, the dustiness that gets everywhere, give the day a migrainous quality. The unremitting street noise is at its most overwhelming in late morning, when the heat of the day has been ratcheted up but everyone's still busy, not yet ready for a lunch break or to sneak a siesta. In those streets that do permit traffic, scooters rev their engines as they weave through the vehicles; high-sided coaches throb a deep bass note. There are queues at the juice stands. Someone is washing the windows of his falafel kiosk;

the glass dries quickly, leaving broad streaky circles. Someone else stands on a ladder screwing a bracket to a house wall. A car pausing at a junction has both front windows down. Loud music from its radio pools at the street corner.

For some, all this is not the beginning of a hundred city stories but a sign that they need to retreat to the ultra-modern, modulated shade of a hotel room and sleep. The unfamiliar food they ate last night and again at the breakfast buffet lies richly in their stomachs. It makes demands that, like those of the street, are just a bit too much for them. They pop a diarrhoea tablet and gaze at their feverish faces in the bathroom mirror, while the aircon hums its international all-shall-be-well lullaby.

How shall we sing the Lord's song in a strange land?

At other times, the city is a jumble of white boxes tumbled into a landscape of tawny brown. Those boxes have been added and added to over the centuries. From a distance it's hard to distinguish between public buildings, apartment blocks and individual family houses. No architect planned the way they interact with the landscape, following its contours and jerkily mimicking the slopes beneath them. These aren't the limestone terraces of an English spa town, nor the smooth lines of some mediaeval French *bâtiment*. Every building seems to be elbowing its neighbour for a perch on one of the city's Seven Hills.

From a distance, in other words, the Holy City looks like nothing more than a jumble of peasant housing. Even the hills themselves don't meet at the Valley of Kidron so much as simply abut each other there. Mount Scopus, Mount Olivet and the Mount of Corruption are three peaks on a ridge running roughly north–south. The lower hills, called Mount

Zion, New Mount Zion, Mount Ophel and Antonia Fortress Hill, lie to their west, completing not a circle but something that resembles a waxing crescent.

All seven form part of the Judean Hills, abruptly stepped, *monocline* formations created in this karst landscape not by gradual dissolution but by a violent geological process: the folding up of the Syrian Arc that started hundreds of kilometres south of here and up to 100 million years ago in the Late Cretaceous period. (How ironic that in Sunday School we did the same, pleating and crumpling sugar paper to imitate these very hills and valleys.)

It's the colours that tell you why you're here. At dawn, on this eastern shore of the Mediterranean, limestone is pink, blue, purple: and each of these colours is merely an inflection of each of the others. So that the melting, shadowy blue of every rock and wall that faces away from the light becomes a delicate, hallucinatory violet, then turns a baby pink that sinks into pale orange. Eventually this colour too will drain away into the pallor of the limestone, but for now it looks as though the stone brims with colour.

We're accustomed to the megalopolis that overwhelms us with its supra-human scale: Shanghai, London, New York. Somehow we expect one of the most famous cities in the world to astonish us in the same way. To be great, we think, it must also be physically greater than we are. The city – or at least that modern megalopolis – has become in our imagination meta-human. We anticipate, even calculate, its unmanageability: too big to be fully known, too bureaucratically complex to understand, too expensive to live in, too loud for thought, too polluted and crime-ridden for free, spontaneous movement.

A city on a human scale, one that measures itself against the individual human mind and body, has come to seem a contradiction in terms.

Nowhere is this more the case than in Jerusalem, a place that three Abrahamic religions believe has been appointed by divine rather than human, judgement; or that must at least reflect divine establishment. Or do they? It's at Babel, not Jerusalem, that the Torah and the Bible picture a skyscraper cosmopolis, while their obsessive detailing of the measurements of the Ark of the Covenant has to do with a portable sanctuary, not city planning. Jerusalem isn't customarily represented in Judaeo-Christian art as having any single, essential form. It's not laid out as some giant symbol, the way the Brasilia of the 1960s outlined an aeroplane in the desert, for example. Islam, of course, eschews representation altogether. But what is believed to be the Quran's City of the Furthest Mosque is not described as having any particular shape.

We forget that 'greatness' might expand into time rather than space. Mecca, Rome, Jerusalem, Delphi, Baghdad: cities that overwhelm us by reputation aren't necessarily either vast or futuristic. True, they have been built and rebuilt to express, as well as to generate, awe. But rebuilding, itself a record of time past, tends to include elements of preservation, so that what we encounter if we make a pilgrimage, even a secular one, to these famous places is a *series* of expressions of awe – of awe transmuted to stone and brick, steel and concrete – each physically and culturally linked to the ones that came before it.

Only destruction breaks these chains of respect. The cities we're most in awe of have been destroyed almost as often as they've been rebuilt. Baghdad, for example, has been repeatedly sacked and reconstructed: destroyed whenever it's most flourishing as if that flourishing itself were what attracted destruction. Which of course is true. No one sets their cap at an insignificant provincial outpost, but caliphates and empires struggle over the powerhouses of civilisation. Even *Roman* Rome was built on the ruins of earlier settlement, then sacked itself in the fifth, sixth, eleventh and again in the sixteenth centuries.

Religious significance makes such a powerhouse doubly attractive. Delphi, a ritual site of Pan-Hellenic importance by the seventh century BCE, changed hands repeatedly and was finally sacked in 83 BCE; in the Roman era it continued to decline in significance until, in the Ottoman Middle Ages, a village was built over it as a final gesture of obliteration – and then in turn removed by archaeologists at the end of the nineteenth century. The limestone city of Mecca, Makkah al-Mukarramah, birthplace of Muhammad and the place where the Quran was first revealed, has undergone radical rebuilding. Structures dating from the time of the Prophet have been knocked down in recent decades to make way for gleaming contemporary facilities – hotels and highways – that seem to reach for hyperbole as if that were the only register fit for a religious site.

The al-Masjid al-Harām, the Sacred Mosque, was damaged by war in the seventh and tenth centuries and by flooding in 1629. Today's courtyard of white, poured concrete roofs, halfway between the canopies of Bedouin nomad tradition and the sail-roofs of the Sydney Opera House, is the product of serial – and still unfinished – renovations by the Saudi royal family, the first started in 1955 and the fourth planned to continue till 2020. These will allow what is already the largest mosque in the world to house 2.5 million worshippers.

Today, the mosque's offical real-time webcam shows the clustering circles of the faithful performing *tawaf*, seven anticlockwise circuits of the Kaaba, or Cube, built of marble, granite and limestone, that is the House of Allah. On a normal pilgrimage day – that's to say outside the annual *Hajj* which takes place in the last month of the Islamic year – two or three hundred white-clad pilgrims pace steadily round the windowless structure. They are neither fast nor slow, but move purposefully and all together. There's nothing subjective or 'expressive' about this deeply meant circumambulation. However modern the mosque that surrounds them, with its escalators and air-conditioning, this is pure practice; an observance that has passed down through the generations and is passing on through today's pilgrims into the future.

Sometimes the Mecca live feed switches to another camera housed in the wide modern arcades with which Masjid al-Harām encloses the Kaaba courtyard. Here, families wander as if through a shopping mall or the transit corridors of an airport. They have the dreamy gait of travellers everywhere, as if shocked beyond astonishment by the sheer enormity of the site and of their journey here.

It was the Romantics who taught the West that awe-inspiring sensory experience moves us and is the measure of us. That rather than reflecting on what greatness means, we can simply *experience* it. It was not the movement's founding belief. William Wordsworth's 'emotion recollected in tranquillity' is a famous call to reflection. But for second-generation Romantic writers, such as Lord Byron and Percy Bysshe and Mary Shelley, awe overtook reason or education as the most profound and reliable form of insight into the world around us.

In Percy Bysshe Shelley's poem 'Mont Blanc', written in 1816, the mountain's 'secret Strength' is its sheer scale:

> Mont Blanc yet gleams on high:—the power is there,
> The still and solemn power of many sights,
> And many sounds, and much of life and death.
> ... The secret Strength of things
> Which governs thought, and to the infinite dome
> Of Heaven is as a law, inhabits thee!

His sonnet 'Ozymandias', composed a few months later, reminds us that giant, manmade structures are merely an aspiration to greatness, and are not greatness itself. But he still uses scale to awe us: 'Two vast and trunkless legs of stone / Stand in the desert' where 'boundless and bare / The lone and level sands stretch far away.'

Highway One (*Kvish Ahat*) arcs through the Judean Hills, descends, and then ascends towards Jerusalem from the west. Beyond the crash barrier, clear mountain light makes the folded rock and dusty gravel on either side of the road appear hyper-real. At 730 metres we're not really very far above the 609 metres that make a British mountain: none of the Judean Hills tops 1,000 metres. Against the pale grey of the desert, olive trees appear surprisingly dark. A pair of raptors I can't name stir the sky, riding a high thermal. As in Shelley's sandscape, 'Nothing beside remains'.

The minibus aircon is on; the radio's been switched off at last. Most of the group have fallen into companionable, jet-lagged torpor. My eyes are dry with tiredness, but my skin feels softened by the mineral-laden air through which we've been walking. I gaze out of the window.

And suddenly there it is again: not shining on a hill, but

spilled down the slopes below us. Not shining at all, in fact, but lightly industrialised; a desert city, built of white stone and off-white concrete.

I recognise this sort of jumble. In the extreme south-east of Spain, the Moorish village of Mojácar is a hectic geometry of whitewashed forms that swarm over Andalucia's final *mogote*, out where kilometres of open scree meet the Mediterranean. There are no streets but only lanes, alleys and stairwells in the settlement's crowded heart. Their twists and turns follow the lost logic of the past. To find your way around, or out, is more a matter of remembering what leads where than of using your sense of direction. So it's always astonishing to emerge on the high plaza at the top of the village, where the church hugs a fortified wall and the flagstones shine smoothly under the brutal blue of the sky.

This village too is built of limestone, and it's set in the limestone of one of Spain's semi-desert regions. Desierto de Tabernas, Europe's only desert proper, is a mere fifty kilometres away. At Mojácar, pyramidal hillocks display strata undisguised by crops or trees, though here and there smudges of tumbleweed and purple toadflax (*Linaria purpurea*) show dark against the rock. Here, as in the streets of Jerusalem, Mediterranean light condenses to a colour sequence in the stone. Desert purples run from deep episcopal to the moiré glitter of a pigeon's wing. At sunset, orange and blue take turns to flush through mile upon mile of stony landscape, dust and prickly pear.

Mojácar was founded sometime around 2000 BCE. Early a trading town, it was part of both the Greek Empire, in the Archaic Period, and the Roman Empire, around 150 years before and after the birth of Christ. It was settled by the Moors when they conquered the Iberian peninsula in 711 CE. From then on, the village expanded and prospered until the fifteenth century, when increasingly bloody conflicts with Christian territorial expansion put paid to that prosperity. Christians massacred Mojácar's population in 1435; in 1488 it submitted to their rule and entered into five centuries of decline, under pressure from drought and consequent poverty. Only since the 1960s have tourism and second homes made the place prosperous again. Still the spatial compromises that this crowded site imposes can seem parsimonious. A house stands partly on the roof of its downstairs neighbour. Another helps itself to a terrace that surely belongs to the house beside it.

But Andalusia learnt many things under the Muslim caliphate: not least the virtues of tolerant coexistence. Mojácans also learnt how to build – even on an exposed hilltop in an unshaded littoral – so as to capture the cooling power of shadow. Today their village retains its Moorish construction. Narrow alleys skirt the zigzag flanks of houses, protected by upper storeys angled to block out a burning sky. Voices echo like rumours in the narrow streets. Everywhere are small cool courtyards, although this was a working village and no palace, and street doors in whitewashed walls lead directly to cool tiled halls.

Across the Mediterranean, and the same village jumble skirts the Acropolis. In the nineteenth century labourers from the small Cycladic island of Anafi, brought to Athens to work on many of the city's great public buildings, built their boxy homes-from-home, island style, onto the steep slope below the Parthenon.

Nearly 400 kilometres away, Anafi is far out in the Aegean, on the southernmost fringe of the Cyclades.

Unlike neighbouring Santorini, which is formed of chunky igneous rock, Anafi is an uncertain, faintly querulous shape. It resembles a jellyfish floating in the blue. In reality it's the tip of a buried limestone range; although the same eruption that created Santorini, and the underwater volcanic *caldera* round which it curves, added some pumice to Anafi's basic limestone and granite.

Anafi is rocky and sandy, bare and beautiful. Today its roughly 250 inhabitants make a seasonal living from tourism. In 1830, when the Greek State was founded, there were no such opportunities. So when, in 1834, the young King Otto moved the capital of the new country from Nafplio to what was then a small town at the foot of the Acropolis, Anafians were glad of the chance to travel to Attica to help build Athens.

Among the great public buildings put up at this time are the University of Athens and the former Royal School of Arts, now the Metsovian Polytechnic, the National Gardens, the National Library and the Old and current Parliament Buildings. Though the usual kind of neoclassical nineteenth-century civic structures that the eye slides past, they carry peculiar freight here where the original, impeccably proportioned Parthenon floats above them on the Acropolis. And down the steep northeastern scarp of that flat-topped *mogote* crowd the houses of the Cycladic islanders who built those replicas. Of whom, first come first served, it was the group from the tiny island of Anafi who named this Anafiotika for their distant home.

Today these slopes are less crowded than they used to be. In the 1950s archaeologists ordered the destruction of large parts of Anafiotika; in the 1970s the Greek State bought up many of its houses for historical-archaeological reasons. Only forty to fifty homes remain, clustered around footpaths whose paving stones are outlined in white. Their gleaming whitewash dazzles at every turn, as if brightness were a competition.

'Small: far away.' In the eponymous TV series, Graham Linehan and Arthur Mathews's Father Ted encourages Father Dougal to understand perspective as together they squint out of the diocesan holiday caravan window at cattle in the rain. The true Anafiotika, 'mini-Anafi', is not Athens' urban settlement, but the island of nostalgic memory.

Back in Spain, Mojácar's indigo doors and whitewashed walls, its red geraniums and Indalo totems, have become tourist kitsch; its desert views and tiled interiors middle-class commodities. Though more commercially successful than ever before, its form has gradually been emptied of meaning. It lacks the content that shaped it. Now the wealthiest settlement in Andalusia, the village has an average GDP four-and-a half times the regional average. But Anafiotika is not empty of meaning. This is still a residential neighbourhood, busy with the pleasures of daily life. There are trees and terraces, old oilcans with geraniums growing out of them, cats asleep on thresholds, and multicoloured flycatcher ribbons hanging in every open doorway. As if to unify it all, lurid bougainvillea climbs on trellises over doors and shutters painted the traditional bright blue of the Greek islands. Sparrows fuss among the leaves in the gutters. Closed between the walls of cottages, the stone-flagged footpaths make acoustic chambers that amplify their cheeping.

Yet Anafiotika's meaning has *changed* since it was built. Today it's not a memory of home but a breathing space in the notoriously polluted city; not the rhythm of life borrowed from an island village but a species of retirement from the bustle of the capital. People still live here, but few today are labourers. Athenian intellectuals are more likely to settle the neighbourhood than the bakers and carpenters who created it.

Now, leaning against the window of the minibus as it circles Jerusalem, you see your own forearm and face afloat on the bright landscape beyond the glass. Under the vast, vague forms of this reflection small figures of roadside hustlers, distant shapes of village houses shift strangely as if they were underwater. They are continually moving away from you. As the road turns they turn too, assume new attitudes. First in profile, next seen from behind. They slide away and they also continue. As do you: sliding vaguely over a landscape that you can't begin to read.

Before we get wealthy enough to hand over to professional builders, we have the practical nous to build our homes from whatever materials are available locally: tile and brick in clay areas, timber in forests. Thatch, for example, is the roofing of choice in regions with lots of reed beds: the English Somerset Levels, northern Romania, parts of China. In places like the northern Danish island of Læsø, eelgrass or *Zotera marina*, a dune grass not dissimilar to marram, is used. Among turf bogs from Ireland to the Ukraine, it's turf sods. So stone, and often whiting too, dominate construction in limestone areas.

Today, fashionable architects try to revive these vernaculars. Yet the forms that delight us are no longer produced by the real pressures that inspired them. They have become cute. Even as we photograph them we wonder whether we really *like* them. Or do we simply admire the sheer necessity that produced them, that makes them 'fit' into their surroundings?

The minibus is parked in a side street under a fig tree, the familiar *Ficus carica*. Though the body of the vehicle's in the shade, the windscreen glares at our retreating backs. Our Israeli guide doesn't want to get out and walk in the City, but she's been faced with a near revolt on board. *We've come all this way.*

She gets her revenge – or perhaps, keeps us safe – by taking us only into the Jewish quarters of the Old City. No Via Dolorosa. No Dome of the Rock. No Mount of Olives. Religious fame, her expressive shrug says, is the most dangerous kind. It's more than her job's worth to pander to Muslim or Christian history.

She's a tightly wound, bony woman with exceptionally mobile shoulders. Her shrug encompasses the fact that our party includes not only European and Asian visitors but also Arab Israelis, Muslim, Christian and Druze. And we aren't easy to control. At every moment one of us lingers, or pauses to haggle over souvenir junk: pierced copper bowls, scarves, postcards. We want, say our lagging feet, to immerse ourselves.

At least we're not hopping and praying and shaving our heads. Jerusalem Syndrome is the most spectacular kind of immersion; a sort of holy high. Its sufferers experience any of the conventional panoply of psychotic symptoms: obsessive–compulsion, delusion, denial, nervous disturbance, hallucination. But in Jerusalem all of these take on religious themes. The medical literature calls this kind of symptomatic translation 'psychotic decompensation'.

Six colleagues from the specialist acute care team dealing with related admissions have published a first-hand clinicians' account of Jerusalem Syndrome in the *British Journal of Psychiatry*. Yair Bar-El *et al* describe, in particular:

individuals with no previous history of mental illness, who fall victim to a psychotic episode while in Israel (and especially while in Jerusalem), recover fairly spontaneously, and then, after leaving the country, apparently enjoy normality. ... Between 1980 and 1993 there were 42 cases fitting the three main diagnostic criteria.

They conclude:

Experience has taught us that improvement is facilitated by, or dependent on, physically distancing the patient from Jerusalem and its holy places. On the whole, major medical intervention is not indicated; minor tranquilizers or melatonin (as in cases of jet-lag psychosis) usually suffice.

Like all such disturbances, the symptoms of Jerusalem Syndrome are oddly literal. Freudians (like the rebarbative, dazzling Jacques Lacan) tell us that, the unconscious is structured like a language; it often seems to be structured like *our* language. In the syndrome, obsessive–compulsion becomes obsessive cleansing of the body, including nail clipping. The desire to visit the famous sites becomes a formal progress to them: one that must be carried out alone and not with friends, family or tour guides – those worldly snares. Possibly my favourite of the seven symptom-stages Bar-El *et al* identify is number four: 'Preparation, often with the aid of hotel bed-linen, of a long, ankle-length, toga-like gown, which is always white.'

'Often with the aid of hotel bed-linen': this is the Jerusalem of the wealthy West, the Holy City of far-away and long-ago;

of Sunday School, of dressing up the kiddies for the Nativity Play in tea towels and old sheets. The syndrome is a Christian phenomenon, and a heavily invested one at that. Of the forty-two victims Bar-El and his colleagues treated between 1980 and 1993, forty were Protestant fundamentalists, one was Catholic, and one was a Jew who had assumed Protestant identity during the Second World War in order to survive.

Can't Jews or Muslims contract Jerusalem Syndrome? The answer appears to be that they don't do so in this individuated, Westernised way. Those Jewish sufferers from related syndromes that the clinicians have encountered are members of small, radical sects, already inclined to odd public behavior. One can only imagine what would happen to Muslim sufferers in the tinderbox atmosphere of Jerusalem's holy sites.

It's as if the self can't contain the significance of the place, and so simply breaks apart. The psyche's like a carrier bag loaded with too many groceries that first splits then bursts as you lift it out of the car. So what is happening here? The researchers conjecture cognitive dissonance. Jerusalem is a modern city, not a first-century-CE town peopled by barefoot shepherds or sandaled regents. True enough: but today's world travellers are sophisticated in the business of antiquity. They know that every site, however famous, will be surrounded by contemporary sprawl.

Besides, the overload of meaning Jerusalem creates is much more like being starstruck than being disappointed. And the dissonance it creates is located within the self. How can *I* have managed to encounter *this*? asks the astonished individual. One response is to take a selfie: here *I* am with George Clooney/the Queen/the Church of the Holy Sepulchre.

Selfies – for all their badly framed narcissism, for all the maddening clutter selfie sticks create across a view the rest of us can't share while they're being used – are acts of integration. Self and other; self in context; me with you, with *this*, with *that*. Without such integration dissonance remains, at the very least as astonishment. It *is* dazzling, awe-inspiring, mind-bending – we have words in every kind of register – to arrive at one of the great sites of the world. The French writer Stendhal knew this. His description of having a panic attack after viewing the frescoes of Sante Croce is famous:

> I was already in a kind of ecstasy from the idea of being in Florence and the proximity of the great men whose tombs I had just seen … On leaving Sante Croce, I had an attack of palpitations, which in Berlin they call nerves; the life was sucked out of me, I walked fearing that I was going to fall down.

Those 'great men' who made Stendhal nearly faint were, he tells us, Michelangelo, Machiavelli, Galileo, Dante, Boccacio and Petrarch. And his account, in *Naples and Florence: A Journey from Milan to Reggio*, makes it clear that it is the reputation of Florence and her culture – *what she means* – rather than any actual quality of the artwork he encounters that so moves him, from his very first sight of the city, on 22 January 1817:

> I saw from far off, like a dark mass, Santa Maria del Fiori and its famous dome, Brunelleschi's masterpiece. 'Dante, Michelangelo, Leonardo da Vinci lived there!' I told myself… Then memories crowded my heart, I felt myself in no state to reason, and I gave into my madness … Approaching the San Gallo Gate with its ugly arch, I would happily have embraced the first Florentine I met.

Stendhal syndrome is something the sufferer brings with him or her. It isn't about beauty: it's about fame.

'*Quel enfantillage!*' – What infantilisation! – Stendhal exclaims. And he's right. Meanings that have the power to disturb us belong to the very structure of our personal world. Religion, learned 'at mother's knee', is a kind of mother tongue that allows us to articulate ourselves to ourselves. The idea that we could *build Jerusalem*, for example – that there could be a society so ideal that it would be existential – borrows the language of religion for its social ends.

Till we have built: in the hymn, William Blake's optimism is set to a famous crescendo by Sir Hubert Parry:

> Till we have built Jerusalem
> In England's green and pleasant land.

'Jam and Jerusalem' the affectionate mock the Women's Institute – for its feminised version of a social ideal, its attempt to dignify the domestic as a collective project. Every WI meeting since its 1924 AGM has started with members singing the anthem that Blake and Parry's 'Jerusalem' has become. But this famously rousing setting was not in fact composed for them. It started life in 1916 to support the Fight for Right campaign for an early end to First World War, and was later taken up by the suffragettes, before local WI branches started to adopt it.

The strange and visionary eighteenth-century message of 'Jerusalem' seems incongruous in its present setting: until you remember that the WI was founded in 1915 to, in its own words, 'revitalise rural communities and encourage countrywomen to become more involved in producing food'.

After the First World War had ended, its mission widened to include women's education and community campaigning. It was in fact a decidedly uncosy, typically Edwardian attempt to do nothing less than build a new society.

Merched y Wawr is the Welsh-language equivalent of the WI, founded in 1967 during another era of social reinvention. It formed as a breakaway from the WI when the older organisation stamped out the use of Welsh. *Merched y Wawr* means Daughters of the Dawn: a name, and a commitment, which in its own way also faces east. Facing towards the sunrise seems so deeply, so usefully, resonant that I wonder what Christians and Jews who live east of Jerusalem, and Muslims who live east of Mecca, make of facing west to pray. Must they adopt a some scrupulously metaphysical doctrine, uncluttered by symbol?

The Macedonian writer Aleksandar Prokopiev captures this sense of the symbolic that halos the east in his story 'Three Aunts':

> On warm days Ditka, my youngest aunt, brought the television onto the west-facing balcony, settled herself to face the setting sun, covered her shoulders with a shawl, and turned her attention to the magic screen. 'Take the Tee-Vee,' she'd say, 'It's the same old trick of the cunning West. Everything begins in the east: the Sun, God, the Letter, the City. But the heat is too much: it turns into conflict, into fire, into slaughter. These things get accepted by the West only when their fury has exhausted itself, when they have become measured and useful.'

Jerusalem glows red and gold in the mediaeval frescoes of Macedonia's early cave churches, carved into limestone bluffs above Lake Ohrid at Radozhda, Kalista, Visni, Struga,

Kaneo, Velgosti, Sveti Naum and Pestani. The city's pictured walls are thick, its arches are delineated with coping stones in matching colours.

Google 'Jerusalem from Highway One' and you see: photos of modern apartment blocks with a background of scrub, aerial views of wide-lane roads curving into lavish junctions, pictures of burnt-out buses and masked men throwing flaming, home-made rockets.

If I forget you, O Jerusalem.

'Highway' isn't a British road category: easiest perhaps to think of this not as a motorway but as what we'd call a trunk road. A motorway network superimposes its autonomous grid of modernity on a country but *Kvish Ahat*, Highway One, is neither autonomous nor modern. A cincture across the narrowest point of this narrow country – the road is barely a hundred kilometres long – it traces a route mapped out by bitter historical habit.

Between Latrun and Jerusalem, it follows the old path over the Judean Hills for fifty kilometres or so. From here the final entry into the city is a steep climb, rising 200 metres in three kilometres. The name, Romans' Ascent, cues its history. This route wasn't paved until 1867, when Ottoman occupiers first laid a road fit for wheeled vehicles. If that sounds like an empire at work, the further widening and paving of the road in 1909–10, simply to make it possible to transport a bell for the German Protestant religious and hospital complex of Augusta Victoria on the Mount of Olives, makes the postcolonial history being played out here clearer still.

From 29 September 1923 to 14 May 1948, this terrain formed part of the British Mandate for Palestine, that transitional 'solution' by the League of Nations to a problem it had set itself: how to change a territory from Ottoman, Islamic dominion into a Jewish free state. In tiny, crowded Israel nothing is innocent and every square kilometre must be contested. In 1948, the Latrun length of the highway, about twelve kilometres, was taken over by Jordan, and non-Jordanian traffic diverted onto a patchwork of roads, Highways 44 and 38, hastily renamed the Road of Bravery (*Derekh Ha'Gvura*). But after 1967's Six Day War Israel reconnected this brief passage through the Occupied West Bank to what had in the meantime been widened to become dual carriageway. At which point the road acquires what on the surface is a more conventional narrative of repeated modernisation and expansion, meaning that it now enables traffic to bypass Jerusalem en route from the coast to Jericho and the Dead Sea, but is of course anything but.

Look up Highway One on the map – or even better, in a satellite photo – and the swirling lines of the surrounding contours show up as roads and settlements. The thick-clustered Israeli settlements with their acres of aligned and shining roofs, and the thinly populated Palestinian villages, neither aligned nor shiny, are alike only in settling along, not against, the lines of the landscape. Hillsides terraced by strata swirl around a limestone quarry at Ma'oz Tzyon, 'Stronghold of Zion'. Hilltop buildings predominate.

Beit Iksa and Beit Surik, along with the seven other villages of the Biddu enclave round which the West Bank border, but not the highway, loops, date back at least to Crusader times. (Beit Surik's Classical Greek remains include a mosaic and Corinthian columns in gleaming local limestone.) Today these villages are famous for having been walled in and separated from Ramallah, which they're forced to reach by fenced-in road and underpasses resembling nothing so much as a literal rat-run. They've also been cut off from their farmland by the West Bank Barrier. Unable to do what farmers must, and access their crops to sow, prune, treat or harvest on days those crops themselves dictate, these countrymen and women have pointlessly – if purposefully – been deprived of their livelihood. And with that go their roots, their dignity and their identity.

Yea, we wept, when we remembered Zion.
We hung our harps upon the willows in the midst thereof.

This is not what Matthew Arnold, in his poem 'Thyrsis', called:

… that sweet City with her dreaming spires
She needs not June for beauty's heightening.

His poem evokes Oxford's limestone towers and finials, architecturally wrought and tastefully set in their local sky. There's nothing spire-like or indeed dreaming about Jerusalem's chunky vernacular. Perhaps what we expect is a white, almost a luminous, city. But Jerusalem is not whitewashed either.

Whiting is the revenge of the peasant on an unforgiving landscape. The headscarfed subsistence farmer with her freshly whited cottage, whether she's Iranian, Ukrainian or Palestinian, is saying no to her environment. No to the dust or mud constantly coming into the home itself, trodden indoors and knocked against doorposts and walls by family home from agricultural labour. No to the heat, that dun-coloured homes absorb and bright-white ones should reflect dazzlingly away. No to germs: one reason dairies are traditionally whitewashed in Northern Europe is that the caustic properties of lime make it a mild antibacterial. No to mess and slovenliness; the lick of bright paint renovates as it protects the home.

Above all, she's saying No to the idea that she is of the earth, earthly. Whiting is a way of distinguishing herself from the soil she lives on and the beasts she lives among: it's her sign of civilisation. It beautifies, and it is also that element of the non-essential that marks her family's subsistence struggle as successful. The woman with a whitewashed home, like the woman whose bedding and other textiles were made with care as she built up her dowry, has achieved a life that's more than brutish chaos.

But whitewash is simply limewash – that's to say lime slaked with water – to which chalk has been added. Whitewash or limewash, both create the whiting that has traditionally coloured cottages across the northern hemisphere, from the West of Scotland to Athens, and from North America to southern Spain. What's the difference? Limewash and whitewash dry to form similar effects but the extra, crystalline shine of limewash is literal, and comes from the calcite of the unmixed lime. Both deflect not only heat but also damp, drying to form a sealant that, though unstable, is at least more watertight than the materials it covers: cob, mud, plaster, lathes, wood.

Whiting looks pretty, especially mixed with pig's blood to produce the pink that typically covers Suffolk pargetting. It's pretty, too, mixed with the laundry blueing that used to do for white washes. *Azurage du linge* – it sounds so much better in the French – produces a range of blue walls, from Atlantic Irish pallor to the characteristic azure of Greek island homes. But the brute chemical facts are basic. It's the addition of chalk that produces the deep glow of whitewash. 'Slaked' lime itself is calcium hydroxide, $Ca(OH)_2$. Unslaked, without water added, it is quicklime – calcium oxide, or CaO.

Quicklime is made by heating limestone or seashells, both of which contain calcium, to between 900 and 1,000 degrees centigrade, and the stone domes of limekilns are a common feature of Western industrial archaeology. The earliest limekilns, on the other hand, were built as cup shapes, their domes formed by the layers of lump stone and fuel arranged on grates for each firing. Lime was raked out from the bottom of these kilns after each firing and cooling, a cycle of about five days.

It was a demanding process, but lime has long been regarded as useful. It's the chemical traditionally used to strip hairs from animal hides in tanneries. It's also the traditional choice of authorities faced with mass burials, especially in times of epidemic. The bodies interred in London's seventeenth-century plague pits were buried with quicklime to speed up the dissolution of their infectious remains. Lime is even a traditional choice for murderers who want to dispose of the body of evidence, so to speak. It was unfortunate for him that the notorious Dr Crippen didn't understand how, while dry quicklime corrodes the things around it, slaked lime does not. After all, if it did, a large number of cottage walls around the world would have burned through. The doctor's purchase of lime shortly before his wife's disappearance not only aroused suspicions about his intentions but, since he mixed it with water, also proved ineffectual in disposing of the murdered woman's remains.

Limewash also protects orchard trees, everywhere from Moscow to Hereford, from sunscald. Scald, which creates long, ultimately fatal vertical splits in the tree bark, is caused by extremes of temperature, particularly the kind that characterise a continental climate. Whiting protects from sunscald but it also keeps the tree cool in spring, preventing too-early flowering and fruiting. Trees with the first one or two metres of their boles painted a grubby white are a typical sight in both the former Austro–Hungarian and former Ottoman territories of eastern Europe.

The scene is repeated over and over at railway halts in provincial Serbia, or on Lithuanian branch lines. The station building is colour-washed, often in blue: we can guess, because blueing mixes so easily with whitewash. A stationmaster stands in the doorway with a flag or paddle upraised for clearance. The low platform is made of cracked concrete. Two mismatched plastic chairs stand near the station door, and one or two fruit trees on whose trunks whitewash is fading cast their shadows onto the track.

It's an old, half-broken dream of order and of plenty, the kind evoked by Yevgeny Yevtushenko's long poem 'Zima Junction', about the little Siberian railway town of his birth. 'Till we have built / Jer-u-salem'. In this dream of social utopia the trains run on time and the 'green and promised land' is so fruitful that no one goes hungry. In Emir Kusturica's 2004 film *Život je čudo*, *Life is a Miracle*, a sleepy railway halt turns into a border post when war envelops former Yugoslavia. Yet its child-like inhabitants continue to try and live the old joyful daydream, drinking slivovitz, swinging in the hammock in the station garden, and falling in love across the new ethnic boundaries. Look carefully and you can even see the whitewash on the station trees.

Approach from the north today, and you can take the train to the old Yugoslav capital of Belgrade via Budapest or Zagreb. Between Vinkovci and Šid the Zagreb line passes through undergrowth so rampant it looks almost tropical: lianas of old man's beard, *Clematis vitalba*, deck stands of coppiced ash and willow long grown out to form astonishing bush-trees. These are uncleared minefields from the wars of the 1990s; less than ten kilometres away is the Ovčara Farm Memorial, site of 1992's Vukovar massacre. Twenty-five years on there are still columns of refugees walking the dirt tracks that cross this border: this time, they've come all the way from Syria.

By contrast, the Budapest train dawdles through the sandy plain of the Banat and mile after mile of vines with not a single person in sight. The black vine roots claw at the sandy soil. Only when the train goes slowly enough can you see that the woody stocks have been painted with a greyish mixture of slaked lime and copper sulphate. (They've probably been sprayed with lime sulphate, too, but that's harder to see.) And still at every stop we see the station master, the plastic chairs and the trees with whitewashed boles.

Matthias Church, *Mátyás-templom*, on the Fisherman's Bastion high above Budapest, is a crenelated Gothic structure, largely rebuilt by Frigyes Schulek between 1874 and 1896. In his reredos for the High Altar, Jerusalem is indistinguishable from the triptych form of the piece itself, each of whose three panels culminates in a crisply gilded gable supported by columns and arcades. Beyond, or inside, these quasi-architectural frames can be seen the carved figures of saints and worshippers ascending and descending wood and gilt stairs, or kneeling to worship in a gilded wooden street.

Transformed by metaphor, the hygienic coat of whitewash that sorts out every spot of dirt and each difficult corner in cowshed or dairy becomes the 'whitewash' that covers every incriminating, adhering spot and difficult corner on the historical, or the journalistic, record. Whitewash doesn't merely conceal: it does so seamlessly.

If I forget you, O Jerusalem, let my right hand forget her cunning.

'Unfortunately, it was paradise', starts one of the Palestinian poet Mahmoud Darwish's great poems of exile. Darwish, who was born in 1941 in the Galilee, died in 2008 in Houston, Texas of that most symbolic of illnesses, heart disease. As a young man, Darwish became famous almost overnight after giving a reading of 'Identity Card', a poem from what was only his second collection, *Leaves of Olives*. Each stanza of the poem ends: 'Write it down: I am an Arab'. The reading, on 1 May 1965 in a packed cinema in Nazareth, caused a near-riot. Within days, 'Identity Card' was being disseminated throughout the Arab world, and Darwish became a kind of Palestinian national poet.

He was always a poet of exile. When he was only seven, his family fled the destruction of their village, al-Birwa, for Lebanon; they returned a year later to live nearby, but in a semi-legal twilight. As a young adult Darwish moved to Haifa, became a member of the Israeli Communist Party and worked as editor of that party's literary newspaper and as assistant editor of the Israeli Workers' Party literary periodical. At twenty-nine, he went to Moscow to study. Three years later, he had joined the PLO, and was forbidden to return home until 1995, when he settled partly in Ramallah.

Being a national poet does not, contrary to British cultural assumptions, mean writing simplistically. Nothing about Darwish's verse is straightforward: apart from the overwhelming impression it creates of a world of beauty and of longing. Sometimes he plays with the gender of his narrator, sometimes with that of his beloved city. It's an ambiguity that makes Jerusalem into something glowing and dreamlike, a dream-symbol that is the more evocative because it is a *ferne Geliebte*, a distant beloved.

But what could be evocative about chalk? Chalk, whose dustiness meant school afternoons, the smear of white dust on the worn-out blackboard, dust smouldering from a chalk-rubber slammed down in anger on the teacher's desk? Chalk that powdered your nervous fingers as you used it when you were called to the blackboard, and that powdered them again later, when you queued to vault the pommel horse in gym?

Though it seems the most institutional of minerals, chalk is a kind of limestone too. This sedimentary rock is formed almost exclusively from the shells, or coccoliths, of deep-sea microorganisms: actually green algae. Their contribution to the biosphere is otherwise of so little interest to biologists that they've been named for their corpses: *coccolithophores* or coccolith-carriers. (On a bad day, one could know what that feels like.)

Chalk – calcium carbonate or $CaCO_3$ – is of course remarkably vivid white. All the same, the famous chalk cliffs disappointed you as a child when, brought at last to see the castle at Dover one rainy day, you saw nothing gleaming and beautiful, no New Jerusalem, just an edge-of-town neighbourhood, murk and greyness. You looked through a penny-in-the-slot viewfinder at the choppy Channel and there was no sign of France. Only a few miles of grey water appeared in the lens, surging sullenly this way and that. The castle was dark flint-stone; darker even than the slate-built castles at home in Wales. The heavily trodden turf outside was more like a municipal park than an area of natural beauty. Squinting sideways into the wind, you could see the next fold of headland, its chalk drop to the shore visible beneath a cap of turf. But the stone appeared grizzled and grey, and the cliffs seemed paltry compared to the Cambrian mountains of home.

You wanted something shining and enormous, the promise of a whole perfect future like in that famous song, '(There'll Be Bluebirds Over) The White Cliffs of Dover'. Even as a child you already knew this 1942 hit: knew it in Vera Lynn's throaty vibrato. 'The White Cliffs of Dover' was something the adults around you whistled and sang and referred to frequently. It was part of their past without you, that mythic era before you were born.

But you heard it as 'bluebells', not 'bluebirds'; and you still think your mishearing was an improvement. Bluebirds make the song into some loose American wish for betterment, for 'Somewhere Over the Rainbow'. (The tune in any case so uncomfortably close to Judy Garland's 1939 star-making solo from *The Wizard of Oz*.) Bluebells, which proliferate on chalk downland like that at Dover, but also in the beech woods that thrive in chalk and limestone soil, would have matched its longing for the war to be over, for the Battle of Britain being fought in the skies above Dover to end, and – the most affecting lines of a song written to affect – for the children lost to evacuation to come home.

And yet chalk is also rare enough, and its whiteness visually odd enough, to be celebrated. The chalk figures of English downland are signs of this rarity: but of what else? Certainly they celebrate human presence and community. The Cerne Abbas Giant in Dorset is visible for miles in the landscape he dominates. So are the White Horses of the North Wiltshire Downs. The oldest of these is the late Bronze Age White Horse at Uffington in Oxfordshire. The chalk figure is in turn younger than the Ridgeway, arguably the oldest road in Europe, which runs along the Downs behind it and on for over sixty kilometres from Berkshire's Goring Gap, where the River Thames bisects the downs, to Overton Hill, just south-east of Avebury and its stone circle. But in 1990, Simon Palmer and David Miles of the Oxford Archaeological Unit were able to date dust from the Uffington horse's muzzle-beak to 3,000 years ago. In other words the figure was created around the time that the oldest books of the Bible and Torah, the Pentateuch, emerged.

Some experts say that the running beast, racing for 120 metres from east to west – sun-wise – along the shoulder of the scarp, is really a cat, and its beaky muzzle is in fact a pair of whiskers. Perhaps because I've always known it as a horse, I have no trouble seeing it as equine. On their coins the local, later Romano-British Dobbuni also portray horses with beak muzzles and limbs that hang below, not from, their torsos. But what astonishes me is the fluent, brushstroke quality of Uffington's giant forms: which could not have been made 'at a stroke' at all, but had to be shovelled laboriously out of the earth. The horse is 'drawn' with trenches of crushed chalk: hard labour, and certainly too much for one person to do alone.

However much earthworks are the *fiat* of a powerful individual, they can be jointly planned and even develop as they go along. Yet a single eye must have 'drawn' the Uffington horse. The creature's boomerang-shaped limbs float below the line of its pommeled back. Its square head flares into two ears; its eye is a dice dot in the centre of that square. Whether

it's a horse, a cat or the white horse goddess Rhiannon –
trace of Celtic religion, who survives in the iconography of
nearby churches like Burford – seems almost not to matter,
now. It is a principle of wild movement. White Horse Hill
dominates the northern landscape for miles, streaking across
the view – from Coleshill for example. Dragon Hill, another
of those conical enormous structures like Silbury Hill – and,
like Silbury, one of King Arthur's reputed graves – stands
at its foot. The White Horse looks as though it has been
released from this mythic burial chamber to race once again
into our imaginations.

Today, the chalk figures of southern England also represent
the continuity of communal presence. Chalk figures don't
stay white. Grass grows over them; grazing sheep erode their
crisp margins. We might expect them to creep and morph; to
slide up or down hill; to broaden or to thin. That they remain
at all is thanks to the annual scouring duties taken on by
local communities. Nowadays, the National Trust organises
educational Family Days at the Uffington site, which it owns.
Traditional scouring activities were more robustly cheerful.
In 1857, 30,000 turned up to drink and watch cheese-rolling
at the Uffington Scouring Fair. Scouring here was first
recorded in 1677 by Thomas Baskerville as an 'obligation'
with festivities as an inducement; by 1720, in *Britannia*,
Thomas Cox was describing an annual Midsummer event
with a highly developed attendant fair.

So chalk figures weren't always quietly mysterious, part of a
landscape of byways and nostalgia. They had a popular, public
heyday in the eighteenth and nineteenth centuries. Over the
border from Uffington, there were thirteen in Wiltshire alone.
Alton Barnes, Broad Town, Cherhill, Devizes, Hackpen, Ham

Hill, Marlborough, Pewsey, Rockley, Tan Hill and Westbury: the names are a roll-call for a half-forgotten region. Some parishes even acquired two White Horses, replacing their familiar figures with improved, 'modern' versions. Many of those created then have since disappeared. Only three of the remaining horses face to the right, in the direction of the Roman alphabet, as the Uffington Horse does; and, since downlands slope in all directions, not all of them gallop west with the sun either.

At Whittlesford in Cambridgeshire, a ghost horse races through the wheat. It can only be seen in aerial photos, because the field containing it is flat. Poor crop growth outlines it: in good years it disappears, like some legendary protector gone to earth. The Whittlesford Society Archive Project has photos from the dry summers of 1999 and 2004 on its website. They show a long-backed horse, with raised tail and doubled rear legs. Its dipped head, with dice-dot eye, abuts a field boundary. The creature appears as a roughly 500-foot-long pallor in the crops: it's even possible that it is a purely natural variation in soil quality. Yet, looking at the photos is strangely moving, like stumbling on some sudden intimacy or a confession.

On the walls of the Templar Commanderie at Cressac in Aquitaine, the Second Crusade continues relentlessly in ochre-outlined frescoes. The twelfth-century Templars gallop and strut around their little Romanesque chapel. Their horses are bay, roan and white, and as tall as the walled and turreted city from which they ride out to engage with Nour ad-Din. Within the city's walls of dressed masonry are a church with a tiled spire, a palm tree, a crenellated tower, and a number of rough-cut inhabitants who look like desperate characters, and who watch the departing horsemen with fierce attention. (The horses however have broad muzzles that, seen two-thirds on, make them look incongruously tame, even a little like wombats.)

The Second Crusade of 1147–9 would have disastrous consequences for both that city and its whole region. In its aftermath the King of Jerusalem, Almaric I, contracted an alliance with the Byzantine Empire to invade Egypt. The invasion was unsuccessful, and the alliance collapsed when the Byzantine Emperor Manual I died in 1180. Salah ad-Din, who had meanwhile become Sultan in 1171, united Egypt with Syria and thus encircled Jerusalem, which capitulated to him in 1187. His invasion of the rest of the crusader states north of the city precipitated the Third Crusade of 1189–92.

Remember, O Lord, the children of Edom in the day of Jerusalem; who said, Raze it, raze it, even to the foundation thereof.

Salah ad-Din was merciful to Jerusalem, by the standards of his time. Though the remaining population were enslaved, and the city's kingdom came to an end, he avoided a massacre, and even negotiated a ransom for many of its leading citizens.

Despite being so distinctive – or perhaps for that reason – chalk, whose Latin name is *creta*, lends its identity to a whole 80 million years of life on earth. The Cretaceous period, when mammals and dinosaurs coexisted and large areas of today's continents were covered by shallow warm seas, ended roughly 66 million years ago. It was concluded by the Cretaceous-Paleogene extinction event, commonly agreed to have been triggered by earth's collision with a bolide at least ten kilometres wide.

That collision created the Chicxulub crater in the Gulf

of Mexico, which is at least 175 kilometres in diameter, 32 kilometres deep, and located just off the Yucatán peninsula near the village for which it's named. An event over a billion times more powerful than the Hiroshima atom bomb, it displaced 200,000 cubic kilometres of sediment and created mega-tsunamis several kilometres high, which swept as far north as Texas and Florida, as well as shock waves that created earthquakes and volcanoes with their own consequences in turn. All of this triggered an impact winter – the dense dust and particulate cloud is likely to have completely filled the earth's atmosphere for several years – which prevented photosynthesis so comprehensively that three-quarters of the earth's animal and plant species, including all non-avian dinosaurs, were wiped out.

This collision with the site's existing carbonate rocks, limestone among them, released a massive dose of carbon dioxide into the atmosphere. The bolide itself would have been vaporised by the collision; but its high constituent concentrates of iridium seem to have passed into earth's atmosphere, to settle with the rest of the resultant debris and form an unusually iridium-rich layer of humus at the end of the Cretaceous period, a point in time and geological space that geologists call the K-Pg boundary.

The effects of the Chicxulub impact seem Biblical in their horror, though since they occurred before the birth of man this is not, for example, the catastrophe handed down in collective memory to become Noah's Flood, or the disappearance of Atlantis. But, since Chicxulub was discovered, craters caused by other collisions which took place in roughly the same era have also been found: the Boltysh crater in Ukraine and the Silverpit crater in the North Sea among them. Emerging in the same period, in west-central India a series of volcanoes known as the Deccan Traps spewed lava and ash clouds capable of creating volcanic winters of their own.

Despite its size, the Chicxulub crater was not discovered singlehandedly, but gradually understood by a handful of engineers prospecting for the Mexican state oil company Pemex. It's a strange story. Those of us who aren't geologists tend to perceive rocks as so brutally large-scale that we assume they must be easily mapped. But the Chicxulub story reveals how geology, whatever its scale – and here it is very large indeed – offers a complex series of codes that take long study to decipher.

In the 1950s, Pemex contractor Robert Baltosser mapped the northern half of the Chicxulub crater arc, but was forbidden by the company to publicise his results. In 1978, company geophysicists Antonio Camargo Zanoguera and Glen Penfield rediscovered the arc and found its southern match. Pemex again forbade detailed dissemination of results and denied Penfield, who became preoccupied with the discovery, access to samples previously drilled in the area. It took the 1990 intervention of journalist Carlos Byars – a non-specialist working for the *Houston Chronicle* – to release Penfield's knowledge. He put Alain Hildebrand, a faculty member at the University of Arizona, in touch with Penfield. In 1980, the father and son team of Luis Walter and Walter Alvarez, from University of California Berkeley, had theorised the possibility of an impact causing an extinction event. Independently in 1981, Hildebrand and his supervisor, William V. Boynton, published their argument that research data (chiefly, rock samples from the Caribbean and the southern coast of North America) indicated exactly this kind of event had indeed taken place. Chicxulub was the missing piece of evidence. Hildebrand was able to get Pemex's permission to analyse rock samples from the site: sure enough, they showed evidence of shocked quartz and tektites, indicating the explosive power of an impact, at the geological layer associated with the K-Pg boundary. That layer was also distorted to lie at a greater depth within the crater site than in normal, surrounding areas. Like the neatly tied-together mass marriage that ends a Shakespearean comedy, the resulting 1991 piece in *Geology*, which in effect announced the Chicxulub extinction event, is co-authored not by one but seven of these key protagonists.

Destruction is a leitmotif of the Mediterranean religions: the Abrahamic traditions and the Classical Greek, Roman and ancient Egyptian pantheons alike. And not only in the Mediterranean traditions. The Hindu deity Kāli is a goddess of both creation and destruction. Islam, Hindu Shaktism and traditional African and African-American religions all embrace animal sacrifice. The principle of sacrifice is pre-Christian in, for example, the whole panoply of northern paganism, Norse, Old Russian or Celtic alike: as Sir James George Frazer's *The Golden Bough*, first published in 1890, famously pointed out – albeit in the unscientific terms of its day.

Deities, however local and numerous, seem to require the expenditure of a life, whether human or animal. *Agnus dei, qui tollis peccata mundi.* 'Jesus's Blood Never Failed Me Yet', sings the old drunk, over and over, in Gavin Bryars's 1971 tape-loop composition. Goats and sheep are particularly popular with the old gods from across the Mediterranean, who can tell a tasty snack from a bit of stringy leftover:

And you shall present with the bread seven lambs a year
old without blemish, and one bull from the herd and
two rams. They shall be a burnt offering to the LORD,
with their grain offering and their drink offerings, a food
offering with a pleasing aroma to the LORD.

This is the Abrahamic God, speaking in Leviticus 23:18, but
he's apparently not the only one to enjoy the smell of cooking.
In Ezekiel 6:13, pagans are also busy cooking:

among their idols around their altars, on every high hill,
on all the mountaintops, under every green tree, and
under every leafy oak, wherever they offered pleasing
aroma to all their idols.

Exile starts with destruction. The new life begins when the
old is utterly broken. In 'The Wanderer', the long Anglo-
Saxon lament that dates from no later than the tenth century:

Gemon he selesecgas
ond sincþege,
hu hine on geoguðe
his goldwine
wenede to wiste.
Wyn eal gedreas!

Here, an exiled soldier is remembering 'the household
knights / and dividing of spoils, / how when he was young
his patron / got him used to feasting. / All joy is dead!' Three
millennia earlier, *Gilgamesh*, which is probably the world's
earliest surviving poem, told a story of orphanhood and exile,
while according to its sixth or seventh century BCE author(s),
before Israel had a king, 'And the men of Judah fought against
Jerusalem and captured it and struck it with the edge of the
sword and set the city on fire.' (Judges 1:8) In Paul Celan's

'Death Fugue', '*Todesfuge*', that great German-language poem of the Holocaust, the destruction is so great that there's nothing left to be remembered: 'Your hair of ash Shulamith'. Only a loss that is absolute, a catastrophe, a *Nakba*, can exile a whole community from Paradise. 'Is that you again? Didn't I kill you?' shouts the soldier from 'In Jersualem', one of Mahmoud Darwish's most well-known laments for the city.

Earth the colour of rust, of fire, of blood. Apt coincidence that here, in Jerusalem, the limestone ground rock should produce *terra rossa* or 'red earth'. In limestone country, heavy rainfall dissolves the carbon from the calcium carbonate of the ground rock, and leaches silicates out of soil that is above the water table. The insoluble residue left behind includes the iron hydroxides which create the rich red colour of *terra rossa*. It's a phenomenon characteristic of karst landscapes, and occurs particularly, but not only, in Mediterranean climates.

'*Terra rossa*', no longer a term used by the Food and Agriculture Organisation, remains in the lexicon of countries, like Italy and Israel, where it's actually most commonly found. Today, with equal literalism, UNESCO and the FAO group this striking soil among the *chromic*, or coloured, *luvisols* ('washed soils'): well-drained soils, where the clay gets washed to some depth. These unusually good drainage qualities make *terra rossa* a dry soil, often characterised by the *garrigue* scrubland that is called *Maquis* in France, and *batha* in Israel. (The name '*garrigue*' itself is another of those karstological terms that derives from Occitan, in which *garriga* means – sedimentary – rock.)

Terra rossa is ideal for wine-growing. It's found in Coonawarra, Australia and in Argentina – both famous for their red wines – as well as in the wine-growing regions of La

Mancha in Spain. Sometimes, rather than a soil it's described as a *rendzina*. This is shallow protosoil or topsoil formed by the weathering of soft, carbonate rocks such as limestone or chalk (or by sulphate rocks like gypsum). Such primitive soil is only halfway to loam: still full of stones and grit. As a result it's noisy to work – it 'chatters' under the plough. Its name comes from *rzędzić*, the Polish for 'chatter'.

The rocks of Golgotha are streaked with red as if something has spilled down them: and it does look like blood. They stand, oddly framed by an iron grill, in one corner of the gloomy Church of the Holy Sepulchre. A cluster of three or four boulders: not a hillside, then. Not the 'green hill far away' that we imagined in Sunday School. The crack running down their flank is said by the faithful to have been caused by an earthquake at the moment of Christ's death. Or it could be a result of the quarrying that, excavations carried out in the 1970s reveal, preceded even the Temple of Aphrodite that stood here originally. The stripy boulders look shrunken and huddled; perhaps that's our surprise. All the same they are quite vividly ugly, and this ugliness calls attention to them even in the church's dim interior.

The Church of the Holy Sepulchre is large but, like the city surrounding it, lacks formal elegance. It takes neither the Roman basilica shape nor the Gothic cruciform. A series of chapels seem simply to have clustered together. That isn't fair to the high-roofed edifice, which viewed from above forms a solid block, with an apse at each end and some supplementary side chapels. However, old territorial disputes over which Christian denominations own the church mean this space is muddled up between the rites: Greek Orthodox, Armenian Apostolic, Roman Catholic (Franciscan), Syriac Orthodox,

Coptic Egyptian and Ethiopian Orthodox. Each has its own dispensation, altar, sacred sites, and in some cases a cordon.

The Church is held to be the site both of Christ's crucifixion and of his tomb, and so of the Resurrection. Unlike other churches in other countries, it isn't merely named *for* those events but believes itself to *be* their actual sites: this accounts for its odd shape. To own the building is therefore by metonymic extension to 'own' the central events of the faith. Internecine Christianity, which has had no trouble spilling sectarian blood as recently as the late twentieth century in the Balkans and Ireland, has turned the odd building which we enter from the corner of a small, sloping plaza into a Babel without a tower. Shambolically, a decree of 1853 which was supposed to put an end to the squabbling between rites ordained that all must consent to any alteration to the common parts of the church: with the result that urgently needed repairs are simply not undertaken. The wooden Immoveable Ladder, still propped where it stood beneath a second-floor window when the decree came into force, is the famous symbol of this impasse.

It wasn't always like this. Earlier worship on the site was marked by transformative zeal. Today's broadly eleventh-century structure was rebuilt in 1048 by Emperor Constantine IX Monomachos and Patriarch Nicephorus of Constantinople, with the express permission of Caliph Ali az-Zahir, whose father had sacked the church forty years earlier. Its semi-crypt is the limestone cave where the early Christians, led by St Helena, worshipped in secret. Unlike their successors, who hang their gold and silver between the pillars, this hidden, first-century community had nothing to leave behind but carvings of a boat, then a Christian symbol, scratched on the bare rock.

Today's shrine is oddly empty, apart from the visitors

queuing at the High Altar. They queue, too, to kiss the stone of the Sepulchre itself, in the marble pavilion of the Aedicule. Its limestone is damp, cool, and shiny with the polish of centuries of pilgrim's fingers. It is also strangely inert. You feel nothing. Clutching your shekels to give to the monk at the little wrought-iron gate of the Sanctuary, all you can think is that the church around you is full of the darkness and superstition of religion gone wrong.

How could this chink of change into the monk's sweaty palm be what lies at the heart of the Mysteries – the Mystery of Incarnation, the Mystery of Resurrection out of that incarnation – that you take to be the life of Christianity? 'Behold, I tell you a great Mystery', the prophet Isaiah sings, in George Frideric Handel's setting in his 1741 oratorio *The Messiah*. Is that mystery really just this fragment of limestone outcrop, this gate of suburban wrought iron, this outstretched palm?

'Next year in Jerusalem ...'

It was Caliph Al-Hakim bi-Amr Allah's destruction of the Church of the Holy Sepulchre in 1009 that gave Europeans the excuse to expel Jews from various of their own cities, including Limoges: Europeans customarily having difficulty in telling non-Europeans apart. The same act became one of the triggers for the First Crusade, which caused further damage to Jerusalem when its exhausted and greedy army captured the city in July 1099, massacring many of its non-Christian inhabitants. By which time the Church had already been rebuilt for half a century.

The song of exile is a song of imprisonment. *By the rivers of Babylon*. It's now almost impossible to read the words of Psalm

137 without hearing a reggae beat behind them. Backing up Boney M.'s 1978 hit are The Melodians, a rocksteady Jamaican band who had composed the Rastafarian setting of the psalm's opening verses nearly twenty years earlier, on the other side of the Atlantic. 'Rivers of Babylon' was the title track of their 1970 album, but it became more famous on the soundtrack of Perry Henzell's 1972 film *The Harder They Come*, which was an international success for the Jamaican film industry. This story about the life and death of a musician-drug dealer was also hugely popular with audiences at home who valued its realism, its use of patois – and the music central to its story.

How shall we sing ... in a foreign land? This ancient song of enslavement and exile speaks directly to Black history in the Caribbean and beyond.

E. M. Forster was no exile, but he was an escape artist. In the novels *Where Angels Fear to Tread* (1905), *A Room with a View* (1908) and *A Passage to India* (1924) he chooses not Jerusalem but Italy and India to explore a type of encounter with the South that, because it delivers a shock to the northerner's system, opens up something – what? An understanding? A way of life? – that's more authentic than the old, unconsidered British way.

For one of his characters, the schoolteacher Miss Adela Quested in *A Passage*, the intensity of this encounter produces, perhaps, hallucination. Miss Quested, who suffers from migraines that take the form of an 'echo', visits the Marabar Caves, where she believes that she is assaulted by her host, Dr Aziz. One of her companions on this ill-fated trip has a related experience:

> For an instant she went mad, hitting and gasping like a
> fanatic. For not only did the crush and stench alarm her;
> there was also a terrifying echo.

It's our own expectations, coming back to meet us, which terrify us.

And sometimes what's longed for and far away is not smaller but larger than it was close up. Psalm 137 has been set repeatedly by musicians in the Christian tradition: by Giovanni Pierluigi da Palestrina in his four-part 'Super flumina Babylonis' and Orlando di Lasso's 1585 motet of the same name, by William Walton in *Belshazzar's Feast*, a setting full of long, longing vowels, and in John Tavener's *Lament for Jerusalem – a mystical love song*, with its chorus of Christian, Islamic and Judaic texts. As a song of spiritual alienation rather than simply geopolitics, it becomes strangely challenging. Instead of a straightforward lament for a lost home, it turns into a confession of spiritual dryness, and the 'waters of Babylon' into more than just the wrong kind of water. In the Judeo-Christian tradition 'living water', the literal translation of the Hebrew for 'fresh water', symbolises life itself. Jerusalem is a desert city.

Many of these Christian settings omit the later verses. The psalm ends badly:

> *O daughter of Babylon, who are to be destroyed; happy shall he*
> *be, that rewards you as you have served us.*
>
> *Happy shall he be, that takes and dashes your little ones*
> *against the stones.*

Hard to admit that fury lies behind longing and belonging. What would you sacrifice for the Beloved? A chicken, a goat? A child?

Let my tongue cleave to the roof of my mouth; if I prefer not Jerusalem above my chief joy.

It's not that the Palestinian–Israeli conflict is irrelevant to Western dreams of Jerusalem. It is that it's of a piece with them. European history is as atrocious as the conflict that rages around Jerusalem today. During centuries of violence, the 'Jerusalem' that Europeans and Russians and Ethiopians and Syrians, Nigerians and Koreans and Americans and Filipinos have called on has been an unreal city. It's a vision of rescue and peace, but also a fantasy of absolute exoneration. The anonymous mediaeval stonemasons, fresco painters and stained-glass makers who represented Jerusalem as a towered city, cinched with a wall like a bunch of flowers tied tight together, were also representing an admonitory principle, a justice that rewards according to service.

The same principle disciplined the believer: *If I forget you, O Jerusalem, let my right hand lose its cunning. If I do not remember you, let my tongue cleave to the roof of my mouth.* This is Biblical justice, of the Old Testament eye-for-an-eye variety. But it's the New Testament Gospels that take up its theme of bodily punishment. In Matthew 5, it becomes part of the Sermon on the Mount, that great setting out of the new religion's stall:

> 29 If your right eye causes you to sin, tear it out and throw it away. For it is better that you lose one of your members than that your whole body be thrown into hell. 30 And if your right hand causes you to sin, cut it off and throw it away. For it is better that you lose one of your members than that your whole body go into hell.

In Mark 9, it's spelled out at Capernaum by the Christ who holds a child on his knee:

43 And if your hand causes you to sin, cut it off. It is better for you to enter life crippled than with two hands to go to hell, to the unquenchable fire ...

45 And if your foot causes you to sin, cut it off. It is better for you to enter life lame than with two feet to be thrown into hell ...

47 And if your eye causes you to sin, tear it out. It is better for you to enter the kingdom of God with one eye than with two eyes to be thrown into hell,

48 where their worm does not die and the fire is not quenched.

In both accounts, Jesus expounds this principle of prophylactic atonement north of Jerusalem, in the Galilee.

The Sea of Galilee shimmers in its limestone bowl in forty degree celsius heat. The delicate green shore contrasts with its rocky surroundings. This green spreads outward through some obviously irrigated orchards, and then traces the valley of the River Jordan, though that watercourse itself is little more than a brutish, muddy drain. If the Kingdom of Heaven is really just on its further bank, it must surely be a castle in this air, which is at once so dazzling and so powdery.

At the shore of the Dead Sea, 429 metres below sea level, average humidity levels notoriously reach 41 per cent in winter. But the Galilee, though also far below sea level, is much less humid. At around 214 metres below, it's thought to be the lowest freshwater lake in the world – unless Lake Vostok, which was discovered in Antarctica only in 1996, turns out to beat its record. Its dry, light-filled air gives an effect of continual optical illusion. The far shore vibrates. Distant details are both delicately clear and ambiguous. A pair of pink-socked black storks, *Ciconia nigra*, roost on a swinging cable; a marsh harrier, *Circus aeruginosus*, slips into the sky.

This is birding country. It lies on the north–south overland migration route from Africa to Europe, and is at the junction between those two continents and Asia. Over 500 ornithological varieties converge here every autumn. So seductive is the Galilee that several species which should be passing through stop here to shelter overnight or to refuel, and simply fail to move on. Rare black storks, though uncommon here as everywhere, do disproportionate, unexpected damage to local telegraph lines. The lake and the land around it teem. Heron, cormorants, spoonbills, ibis, cranes, storks and egrets wade the shallows, and there's rich variation within the species. Here, heron aren't simply the tall grey fisher-birds, *Ardea cinerea*, that we recognise from English watermeadows, but also the subtly coloured purple heron, *Ardea purpurea*, the night heron, *Nycticorax*, and squacco heron, *Ardeola ralloide*. While various species of warbler, wagtail and kingfisher hop in the reedy undergrowth, among the raptors, owls, harriers, eagles and vultures add a note of threat to the skies with their bulky silhouettes. The imperial eagle *Aquila heliaca* makes itself at home: as do Bonelli's eagle, *Aquila fasciata*, and the short-toed eagle, *Circaetus gallicus*. One of the largest raptors in the Galilee is the griffon vulture, *Gyps fulvus:* its wingspan can exceed two and a half metres.

Paradise for birds, but living here isn't always so easy. The Sea of Galilee formed in the Jordan Rift Valley, in what's theoretically the northern part of the Great Rift Valley. This remains earthquake country; the last major shake was in 1837.

It's also a storm corridor. Low-lying and surrounded by hills, the lake is prone to sudden squalls, as Matthew 8 once told all Christendom:

> 24 And behold, there arose a great storm on the sea, so that the boat was being swamped by the waves; but he was asleep.
> 25 And they went and woke him, saying, 'Save us, Lord; we are perishing.'
> 26 And he said to them, 'Why are you afraid, O you of little faith?' Then he rose and rebuked the winds and the sea, and there was a great calm.

The lake's shore is overlooked by the Golan Heights. I was a child in 1981, when the Heights were annexed by Israel. I remember the serious voices of BBC newscasters as they talked through the crisis and discussed 1973 and 1967, that grim chain of consequences. *Go-lan* sounded onomatopoeic with threat. The Heights I imagined then were doomy and dark, cliffs probably made of granite, certainly not this limestone ridge afloat in a blue sky. My dreams, during those weeks, were a confusion of the London giants Gog and Magog, of golems, and of robotic, helmeted soldiers.

But today, as the minibus strains over the shoulder of the last rise, the blue lake below us is a smudge of colour among the ochres, whites and yellows of the bare hills. On satellite photos these limestone pigments swirl brilliantly with the rise and fall of contours. These aren't the colour-keys of the world's national geological surveys; instead, the tumbled, organic colours of the actual geology appear almost edible. The Judean Hills resemble those fabulous ice creams that used to be made only in Italy but are now sold everywhere: caramel swirl, honeycomb and chocolate, nut crunch brittle.

And swirl they do. Does this appear such a territory of great forms because the hills are bare; or because they're the outcome of a radical folding up of the landscape? The Judean Hills are part of the Syrian Arc, whose giant letter S through Syria starts in the Sinai Peninsula, passes through the Negev Desert and runs on to the Palmyrides just south of the Aleppo plateau. To create such a sequence, the direction of stress must have wandered. Some of this wandering, especially in the Palmyrides, may have resulted from a collision between the Arabian plate and the Anatolian sub-plate, around the time of the Dead Sea Transform in the Neogene Period between 23 million and 2.6 million years ago; other directions of fold appeared through pre-existing faults.

The contours take on different aspects as we descend. Now they seem less like ice cream than the languid curves of human bodies. The road doodles round these as if for the pleasure of tracing them. These colours are shifty, subtle inflections of each other like the is-it-isn't-it colour on a jay's wing as it tilts in flight, or the hair-by-hair variation in the fur of a tortoiseshell cat. As they pass into and over each other they appear to form an intimate and easily manageable landscape. These are not mountains that shout *Danger!* Tempting, too seductive, they're a landscape meant for wandering and settling, wandering and settling; a geography one could fall in love with.

But today, as the intifada enters another year, there are no tourists ogling the Judean Hills. The beach where Tel Aviv's skyscrapers give way to the low stone houses of mixed, Arab-Israeli Jaffa is deserted. No one's making a fortune shepherding Born Again Americans around Bethlehem and Nazareth. And nobody on this minibus has made the decision to come here lightly. (Only a project like this one, pushing for dialogue in the strongest of senses, could have fetched us in.)

Yet it's the landscape of our dreams, and of the dreams of the countless generations who never made this journey: 4,000 kilometres from Tourtoirac, 3,500 kilometres from Škocjan, 5,150 kilometres from Coleshill, 20 kilometres from Ramallah.

If I forget you, O Jerusalem. The light makes everything dreamlike. There's haze: a dustiness settling at the bottom of the sky. In this version of limestone country, it's impossible to see anything perfectly clearly. Still, the light says: hope. What can we do but hope? From far away, it is what Jerusalem represents. For those who live at closer quarters, that hope is mixed:

> In Jerusalem, and I mean within the ancient walls,
> I walk from one epoch to another without a memory
> to guide me. The prophets over there are sharing
> the history of the holy … ascending to heaven
> and returning less discouraged and melancholy, because love
> and peace are holy and are coming to town.
> I was walking down a slope and thinking to myself: How
> do the narrators disagree over what light said about a stone?
> Is it from a dimly lit stone that wars flare up?
> I walk in my sleep. I stare in my sleep. I see
> no one behind me. I see no one ahead of me.
> All this light is for me. I walk. I become lighter. I fly
> then I become another. Transfigured. Words
> sprout like grass from Isaiah's messenger
> mouth: 'If you don't believe you won't be safe.'
> I walk as if I were another. And my wound a white
> biblical rose. And my hands like two doves
> on the cross hovering and carrying the earth.
> I don't walk, I fly, I become another,
> transfigured. No place and no time. So who am I?

I am no I in ascension's presence. But I
think to myself: Alone, the prophet Muhammad
spoke classical Arabic. 'And then what?'
Then what? A woman soldier shouted:
Is that you again? Didn't I kill you?
I said: You killed me ... and I forgot, like you, to die.

'In Jerusalem' by Mahmoud Darwish
translated by Fady Joudah

Acknowledgements

Grateful acknowledgements are due to the *King James Version* 2000 of the Bible, from which all the italicised quotations from Psalm 137 in 'Unreal City' are taken. Other Biblical quotations are from the *English Standard Version*. I am grateful to Curtis Brown for permission to quote from W. H. Auden's 'In Praise of Limestone' and to Ed Victor Ltd for permission to quote from Stephen Spender's 'The Pylons'. Most of the translations that appear here are my own, and any infelicities they may contain are my responsibility. The exception is 'In Jerusalem' by Mahmoud Darwish, translated by Fady Joudah, for which I'm grateful to Copper Canyon Press for permission to quote. I'm also grateful to Alesandar Prokopiev for permission to quote from my own translation of his story 'Three Aunts' and to Andrej Brvar for permission to quote from my own translation of his poem 'A Small Odyssey'. My translation of Dante's *Inferno* is from Canto III lines 56–7.

The statistics on Slovenian housing are taken from European Commission, Eurostat *Housing Statistics: Tables and Figure*. I quote from the paper on Jerusalem Syndrome by Yair Bar-El, Rimona Durst, Gregory Katz, Josef Zislin, Ziva Strauss, Haim Y. Knobler, 'Jerusalem Syndrome' in *The British Journal of Psychiatry* Jan 2000, 176 (1) 86–90; DOI: